# Essentials of Circular Machine Knitting

# ESSENTIALS OF CIRCULAR MACHINE KNITTING

## Lucy E. Best

Best Gearhart Knitting Machines
Brasstown, North Carolina

Essentials of Circular Machine Knitting

Copyright © 2018 Lucy E. Best

First Printing, 2018

All rights reserved. No part of this book may be reproduced in any form, except for brief excerpts for the purpose of review, without written permission of the author, Lucy E. Best.

Published by:  Best Gearhart Knitting Machines
              61 Best Way
              Brasstown, North Carolina 28902

Cover design:  Lucy E. Best
Book design:  Lucy E. Best
Photography:  Lucy E. Best
Technical assistance:  Elizabeth Love

Printed by CreateSpace, an Amazon Company

ISBN10:  0-9859369-3-2
ISBN13:  978-0-9859369-3-8

*To Florence Cooper Best,*
*my great aunt,*
*whose book manuscript, the work of her lifetime,*
*was lost a few months before it should have been published in 1958.*

# TABLE OF CONTENTS

1. Table of Contents..................................................vii
2. Introduction..........................................................ix
3. Author's Note........................................................xi
4. Before You Begin..................................................13
5. Starting the Web...................................................17
6. Buckle and Weights...............................................29
7. Stitch Size or Tension Adjustments..........................33
8. Gauge Swatch.......................................................35
9. Selvedges for the Beginning....................................41
10. Bottle / Can / Ice Cream Sleeve................................47
11. Reversing and Short Row Heels...............................49
12. Cylinder Markings..................................................51
13. Weighting the Heel.................................................53
14. Short Row Heel with Wrap on the Increase...............57
15. Drawstring Purse or Marble Bag...............................67
16. Cord......................................................................71
17. Tuck Stitch Top Stockinette Sock..............................73
18. Tuck Stitch Top Mock Rib Sock................................75
19. Hung Hem Top Stockinette Sock..............................79
20. Hung Hem Top Mock Rib Sock.................................81
21. General Tips..........................................................85
22. Terms and Definitions.............................................87

# INTRODUCTION

Begin your circular knitting machine journey by mastering four essential skills: starting a web on the machine, adjusting the stitch size, creating a selvedge, and reversing. Establish a solid foundation to allow you to create socks and other items at home. Intermediate knitters may find this a helpful review to improve overall success.

These instructions, originally developed for a weekend class, have been revised and expanded so that they may be used as a stand-alone, self-guided introduction to the hand cranked stationary cylinder circular knitting machine *capable of reversing*. There are many new and vintage machines of this type in use today. Much of the general information will also apply to the hand cranked rotating cylinder circular knitting machines or can be adapted for use with them. Plastic hobby and children's hand cranked circular knitting machines which only knit in one direction do not have the same capabilities or design features as these more advanced machines, so this material is not intended as training for them.

The ribber assembly will not be used for this experience (although occasional references to it have been included).

# AUTHOR'S NOTE

There are two basic philosophies in the teaching of circular knitting machine techniques. One approach is to teach the elements of the process with limited variables and ample opportunities for practice. Skills build sequentially. Focus is on the process rather than the product. The student may not produce a wearable sock immediately, but the elements necessary to create socks have been mastered. The second approach is to guide a student one step at a time through an entire sock, making immediate corrections to the product, with the goal of a sock. In this approach, the instructor usually sets up the project so that it will be successful with the appropriate yarn, delivery system, tension, and pattern. The student does complete a sock but may have no idea how to accomplish the same thing independently. More time may be spent correcting a mistake than developing a successful technique. Neither approach is perfect for every student or every instructor. I choose to present the mastery process.

There is often more than one technique available to create a desired result with these machines. In general, I have provided the option I have found to be the most useful to students using a variety of machines, vintage and contemporary. This is not always the method that is the fastest or has the least steps, but it is usually the one that produces the best initial success in a group setting. These techniques should work on all of the common stationary cylinder machines in good condition, regardless of model or make. Some of this will come very easily; other elements will require practice. Expect to spend some time acquiring these skills. However, if a method offered here does not work for you after several serious attempts, be aware that there may be other options not covered here.

You will find information about process followed by one or more projects designed to build the skills covered. I suggest that you work through these in the order they are presented. Spend a fair amount of time practicing heels to master this element before trying to create a heel that is incorporated into a project. You have permission to give up on a snarled mess or a section with lots of runs. Move on. Knit a length of waste yarn so that you have a solid foundation above the buckle and weights, and try again. Do not spend hours trying to resurrect an area with a significant error. Start over and work to master the correct technique. Yes, it is possible to fix runs on and off the machine. It is useful information for the long haul, but it is better to learn to knit without runs.

At this stage, use the suggested practice yarn and do not focus overly much on the size or texture of the resulting product. Choose a stitch size at which the machine will knit the practice yarn easily. Adjustments in materials and stitch sizes can come later, after you have mastered critical skills.

The final four sets of instructions put together multiple skills to knit basic socks. Do not throw out the earlier principles you have used when you get to these patterns. These are *practice* socks. It is tempting to change the yarn, change the tension, and change your expectations when you get to these. Please do not. Knit these socks without prejudice. Get used to the sequence necessary to put the parts together and to plan ahead for the next element. Be willing to scrap an attempt which is not working well and start over. Continue to focus on the process and master the steps.

I hope you will enjoy your journey and have many happy and successful projects.

*Lucy*

Brasstown, NC
2018

# 1. BEFORE YOU BEGIN

Make sure your basic machine is complete and that all parts move appropriately. This material assumes that your machine is tuned so that it can form stitches correctly.

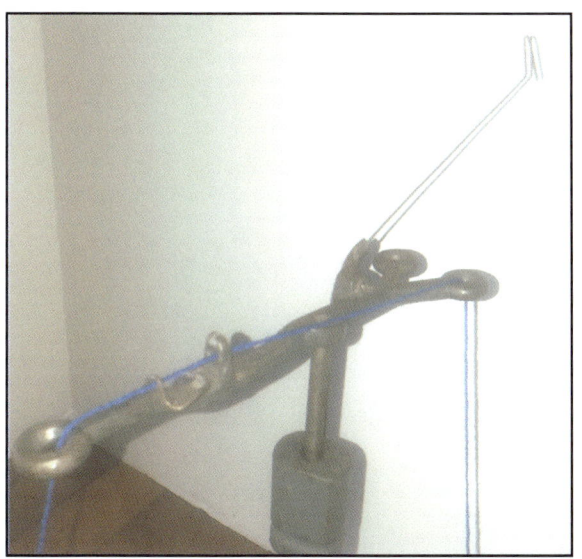
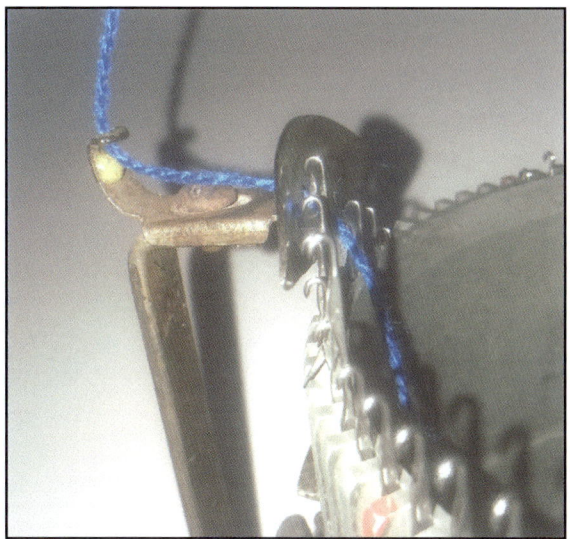

Find a threading diagram for your machine if you are attempting this solo. Although features vary a bit, most threading is quite generic. There is one unusual mast top which was originally sold with some of the Canadian machines that may require specific instructions. There is no common name for this top—it has two eyelets in the back but is lacking the usual third eyelet over the center of the machine. The heel spring is tensioned by a spring wound down around the mast. I have noted disagreement among contemporary users about the correct threading for this design, so do not be surprised if you find conflicting information.

You will also need to identify the tension adjustment knob or nut on your machine. This part is turned to change the size of the stitches by raising (smaller) or lowering (larger) the tension or V-cam. If your machine has a knob adjustment, a clockwise turn will make the stitches smaller while a counterclockwise turn makes them larger. If your machine has a nut, a clockwise turn will make the stitches larger while a counterclockwise turn makes them smaller. We will explore the range of settings of your machines in one of the activities, but you will need to be able to locate and adjust the tension to the middle of the range to begin any knitting.

If you have multiple cylinders, choose the 54, 60, 64, or 72 when possible. These tend to be the most useful to beginners. The very coarse cylinders (fewer than 54 slots) and the very fine cylinders (more than 72 slots) present additional challenges.

Identify and obtain the correct needles for your machine. New needles are not essential; but good, functional, smooth needles are. All your needles should match in design and dimensions. Beginners often find it difficult to separate problems arising from bad needles from issues of poor technique. Good needles are worth the investment.

Collect all necessary accessories. At the very least, you will want some sort of pick/hook tool, a stem weight, a buckle or similar device to attach the weight to the web, scissors, a large eye yarn needle, and a set up bonnet (The number of stitches is not critical.) It is also prudent to have your machine lubricant and adjustment tools within reach. A pen and paper may also be useful.

Put your machine on a stand or table that is an appropriate height. In general, the pivot point of the crank should sit at or just below your elbow. The cranking motion should move the forearm up and down at the elbow and the upper arm back and forth at the shoulder. Most people prefer to sit; the occasional knitter chooses to stand. Either is fine, but the feet should be able to rest flat on the floor for the best back support. A tall chair or stool used to accommodate an overly high stand usually precipitates low back stress. A table which is too low will also stress the back. A table which is too high is likely to affect the shoulder and neck.

Position the machine so that the arm powering the crank has a back and forth movement rather than a side to side movement. It will be necessary to offset the machine so that the mast is slightly to the left of center as you sit. These machines were designed in an age when ergonomics were not often considered, and the angle of the crank demonstrates a lack of understanding of repetitive motion injuries.

Do not practice with yarn that is precious to you. For all intents and purposes, you will need to be able to consider this practice yarn disposable.

Choose an inexpensive practice yarn that is a little finer than the average sock yarn appropriate for your choice of cylinder. Specific recommendations will be included at the end of this section.

A generous quantity of yarn (a pound or more) on a commercially wound cone is recommended. You will need two similar yarns (two cones) in contrasting colors. Contrasting colors are important so you can identify the waste yarn from the project yarn. There are many uses for this practice yarn beyond these initial activities, so do not be concerned about having too much yarn. Rewinding and/or reusing yarn changes its character and affects the way it knits. You will want to explore yarn delivery systems (cones, bobbins, balls) and preparation techniques as you progress, but it is not necessary to add this to your initial beginner burden. Commercially coned yarn allows you to focus on fewer variables as you develop your basic skills.

Acrylic and wool yarns or blends of the two are suitable. If using wool, examine the cone for damaged areas. Wool that has been attacked by insects will cause a great deal of frustration. Avoid cotton, linen, tencel, rayon, and specialty fibers at this stage.

Choose a yarn which is a consistent weight without loops or excessive fuzz. Avoid slippery yarns —those which slither off the cone if not stabilized.

Yarn weight descriptions vary from system to system and are often inexact. Rather than trying to master this element now, look for practice yarns that meet these criteria in addition to the previous suggestions:

**For cylinders with 48 to 72 slots, look for a yarn identified as approximately 2200 yards per pound. Tamm Yarns' Bebe line is in this weight range.

**For cylinders with 72 slots or more, look for a yarn identified as approximately 2400 to 3600 yards per pound. Tamm Yarns' 3 Ply Astracryl should work on most higher count cylinders.

## 2. STARTING THE WEB

For the machine to make new knit stitches, each needle must be provided or develop a base loop. The set up bonnet is one accessory which can provide this initial loop. It is inexpensive to make, easy to use, and easy to replace. Many machine sellers provide a bonnet when a machine is sold. Bonnets can be purchased online and elsewhere.

It is common to choose a set up bonnet made on the same number of needles as those in the cylinder, allowing every other needle to be looped for the initial pass; but this is not essential.

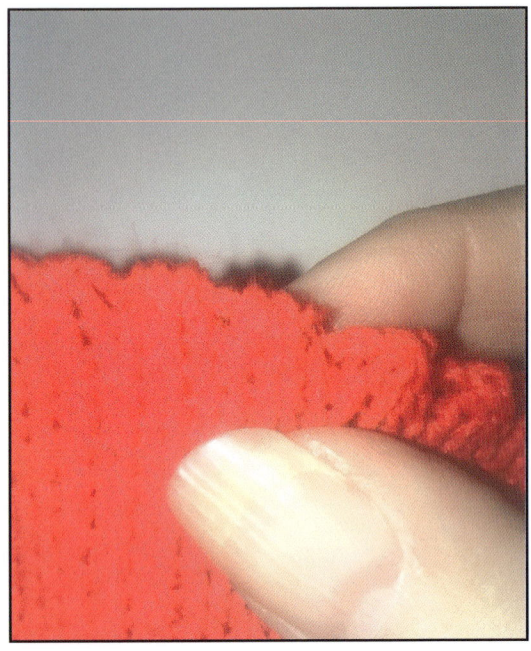

The very basic set up bonnet has a picot edge which offers stitches and floats which can be looped over needles. Other bonnet patterns incorporate an additional looped line, specialty yarns, jump rings, and other adaptations. These instructions will explain the use of the common bonnet.

Before hanging the set up bonnet on the needles, raise one needle at the front of the machine so that the butt is resting against the cylinder spring. Knit forward to position the yarn carrier at the front of the machine. Move the carrier gently while there are no stitches on the machine. Latches from empty needles can be out of position at this stage. *From this point on, do not turn the crank backwards for any reason.* Center the carrier below the raised needle. Thread the machine mast and yarn carrier. Position the source yarn cone on the floor, and make sure it can unwind freely.

Set your machine tension in the middle of the tension range. You may need to refer to a manual or other resource to understand the tensioning system for your machine. Identify the adjustment nut or knob, turn it in one direction until it can not turn any more. Then turn it in the opposite direction, counting the number of full turns, until it stops again. Divide the number of full turns by two, and make that many turns back to the approximate center of the range. This should give you an adequate stitch size for starting the machine with the practice yarn. This does not have to be exact.

Hold the set up bonnet inside the cylinder with the picot edge near the needles. The picot edge will be uppermost and the other end of the bonnet will be lower. The mouth of the bonnet, the picot edge, will follow the curve of the cylinder on the inside edge.

Place a loop from the top edge of the bonnet over the first needle behind the right half mark.

The loop may be a float between the bumps of the picot edge or it may be one of the stitches which form the picot bump.

Skip one needle in the knitting direction (counterclockwise from the right half mark). Hang another loop from the bonnet on the 3rd needle.

Skip another needle in the knitting direction. Hang another loop from the bonnet on the 5th needle.

Continue this process as far as you can around the cylinder until you reach needles that are not accessible.

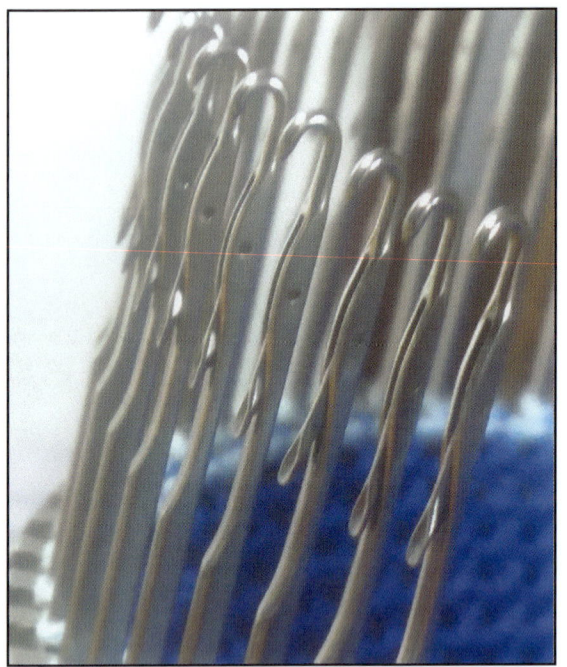 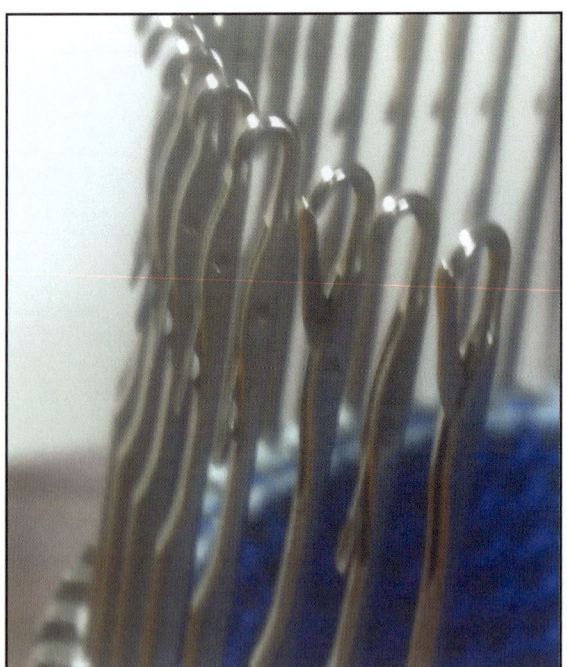

Inspect all the needle latches to make sure they are open. An open latch means that the tongue is pointing downwards so the hook of the needle is not blocked. A closed latch has a tongue pointing upwards so that the hook is blocked.

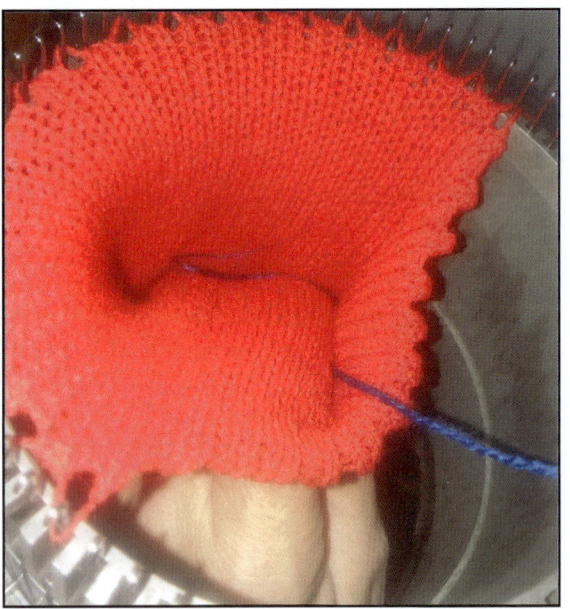 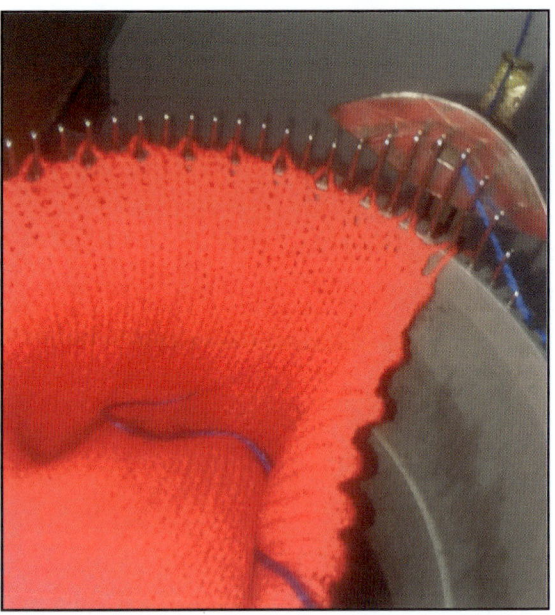

When you have hung as many loops as you can, tuck the tail end of the yarn down inside the bonnet and pinch it (reaching up underneath the machine with your left hand) to prevent it from being drawn backwards through the yarn carrier. If you turn the yarn carrier without yarn in it, the loops of the bonnet that you bypass will drop and will have to be rehung.

Slowly turn the machine crank to begin the knitting process while gently pulling downward on the bonnet. This tension must be continued at all times, either by your hand or by weights, for the machine to knit correctly.

As you move to knit this first pass, the raised needle can be lowered just before the yarn carrier arrives at the right half mark.

Knitting forward will raise the needles that were not available when you hung the first section of the bonnet. Complete the loop hanging process until you have returned to your starting position. Advance the yarn carrier as necessary to accomplish this, remembering to hold down on the bonnet each time the carrier is moved.

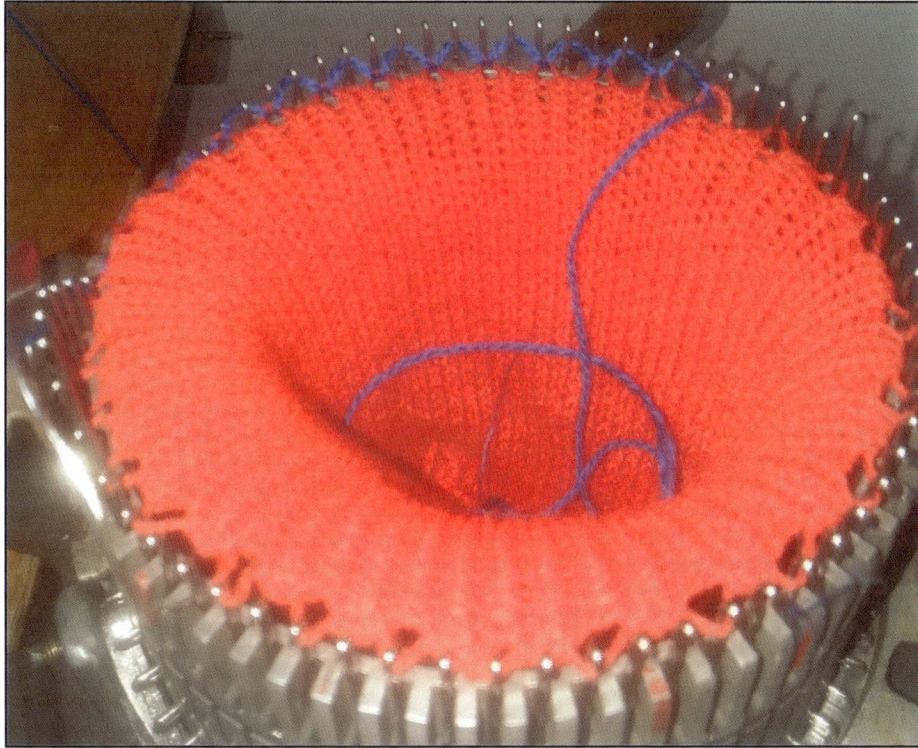

The bonnet loops should be cast off as new stitches, formed from waste yarn, are created. Needles which did not have a bonnet loop should acquire a waste yarn loop on the first or second pass.

Do not be concerned if all needles do not begin knitting immediately. Confirm that the latches of the empty needles are open.

Continue holding the bonnet down with your left hand while turning the crank with your right. If you are pulling straight down, most machines will eventually begin knitting on all needles.

Most bonnets have some method of supporting weights, either internally or externally. You can choose to use weights to provide the downward pull, but it is wise to develop the habit of keeping the left hand on the web when knitting in addition to weights. This allows you to feel normal and abnormal machine function.

If you have knit several rows and some needles refuse to knit, you have a number of options:

**Pick up the float between the adjacent stitches and loop it over the empty needle. This may be enough to get the needle knitting on the next pass.

**Pick up a nearby stitch from a previous row and hang it on the empty needle. This should also allow the needle to begin knitting normally.

**Raise the empty needle out of work, knit past it once, return it to work, and continue knitting. This has the same effect as adding a loop to the needle.

If two or more adjacent needles are not knitting, address one of the needles with any of the previous options until knitting is established on it. Then move to another non-knitting needle.

If one or more needles refuse to work after attempting these steps, examine the needle(s) carefully. Does the needle *have* a latch or tongue? Does the latch open and close easily or does it have a slight hesitation when it is moved from the open position towards the closed? When closed, does the tongue of the latch hit the needle hook squarely, or is it bent off to one side or another? Does the needle match the other needles in the machine? Is the needle rusty or dirty? If you see anything unusual, replace the needle and try again.

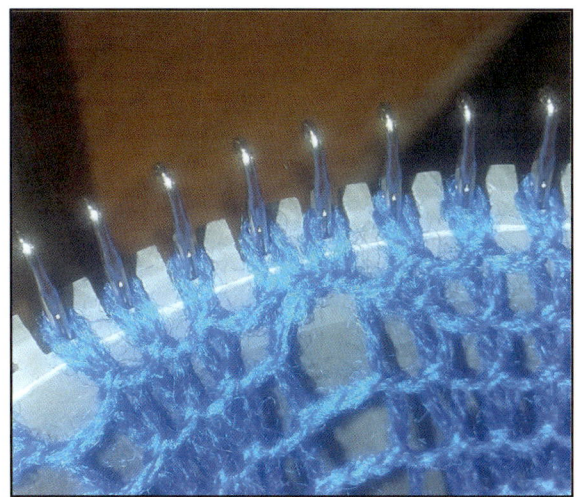

Look also to the downward pull on the non-working needle. Shifting the tension on the web by repositioning your hand or finger may increase the pull on the affected area and allow the needle to begin knitting.

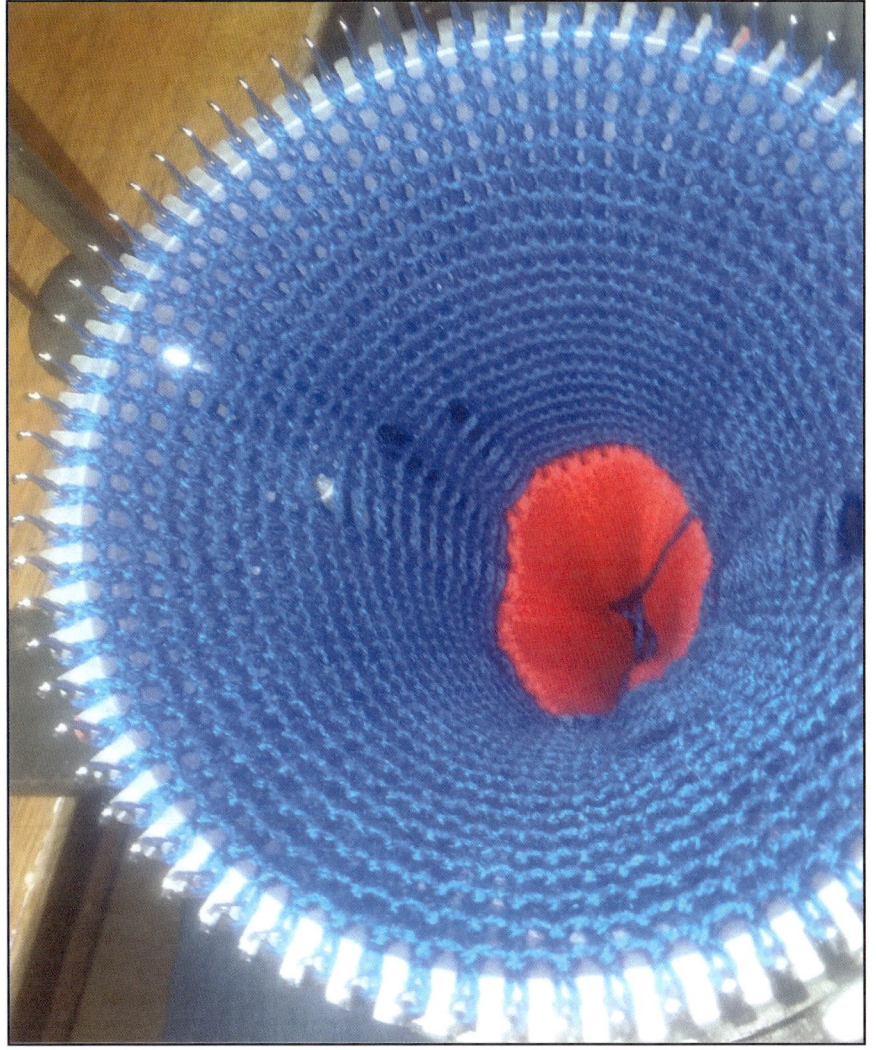

Once all needles are knitting, add enough rows of waste yarn web so that the buckle and weights can be applied. The set up bonnet start often provides uneven tension and is not always a good foundation for a project. Develop the habit of adding the buckle and weight before attempting any project or technique.

If your machine is difficult to crank or is making any form of grinding noises, stop and evaluate the machine for tensioning, tuning or assembly problems. The problem may be inappropriate stitch size relative to yarn size, poor positioning of the yarn carrier, no pull down on the web, damaged needles, incorrect threading, snagged yarn, loose cylinder screws, incorrectly inserted cylinder, and more. If needles break, you have a tuning or tensioning issue or both. ***Stop and evaluate the machine. Something is wrong***.

A bonnet made with a picot edge usually has half the number of loops as the number of needles used in the cylinder which created it. This may be slightly more or less than the number you need to catch every other needle on your own cylinder. If you have more loops in your bonnet than half the number of your needles, skip a loop every once in a while to space the bonnet more evenly. If you have fewer loops than half your needles, use the 3$^{rd}$ or 4$^{th}$ needle every once in a while instead of every second needle. This will not matter greatly. You are using this bonnet as a tool to get the machine started with waste yarn. It will *not affect* your finished product unless you forget the essential buckle and weight step before you proceed.

When this section of tube is removed from the machine, you should be able to clip a few loops of the first row of waste yarn knitting and remove the bonnet intact and ready to be used again. If loops or stitches of the bonnet break, choose another section of the knitting to provide a loop. Bonnets can become quite raggedy and still provide enough loops to get a machine started.

# 6. BUCKLE AND WEIGHTS

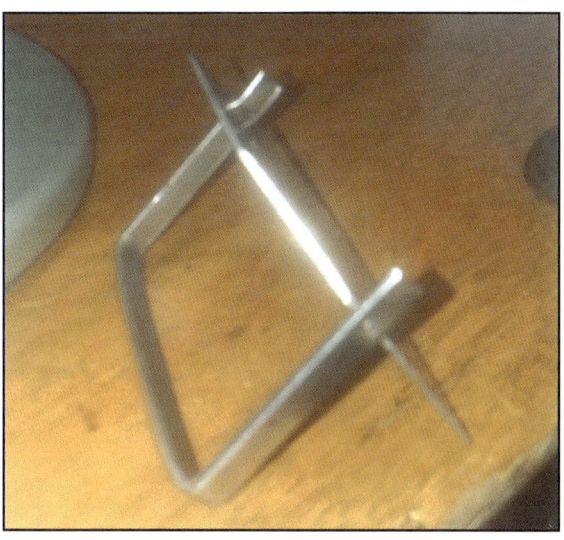

To apply the buckle, hold it with the loop end or the hole for the weights at the top.

Allow the hinged bar to swing away from the body of the buckle.

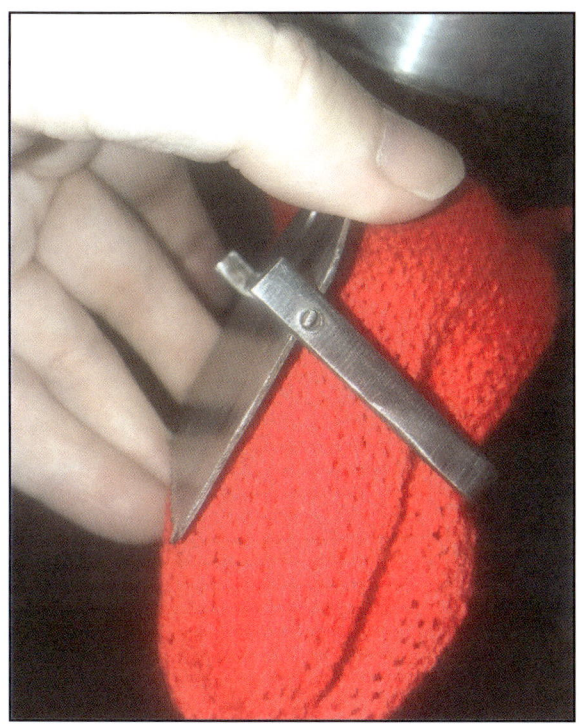

Keeping the entire buckle upright this way, slide the web (your tube, sock, or bonnet) down between the bar and the body of the buckle.

Slide the buckle up as far as you can onto the waste yarn.

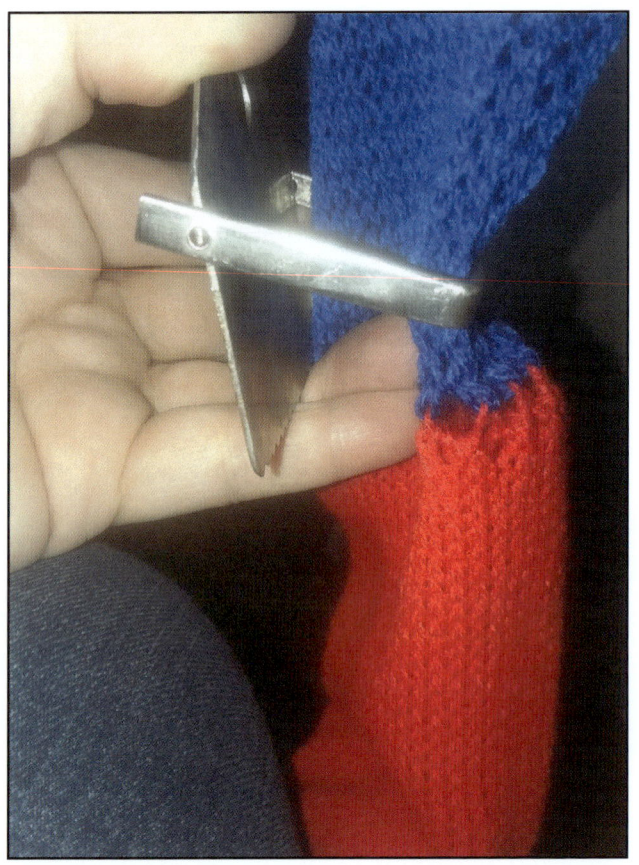

Now invert the buckle so that the loop end or hole is at the bottom of the buckle. This should cause the web to fold back on itself in the jaws of the buckle. Make sure the web lies evenly and is not bunched at one end.

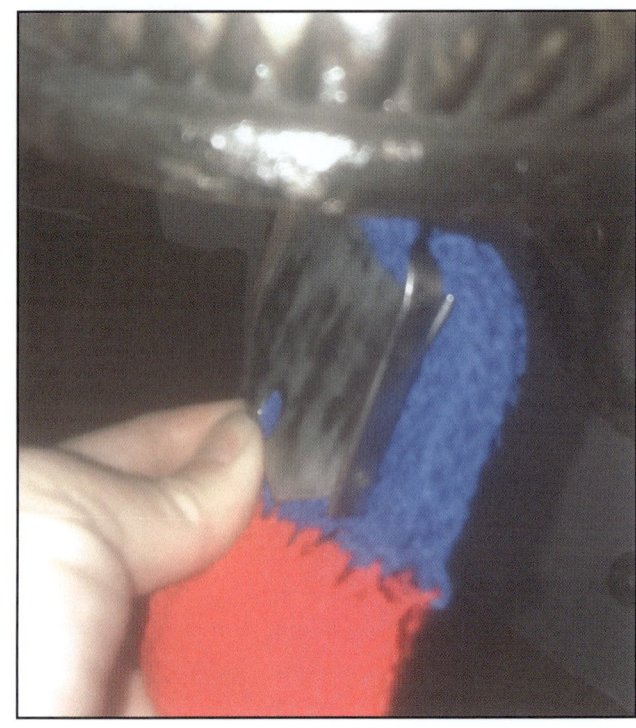

The weights can now be attached.

The buckle can be raised by pulling up on the lower end of the web where it exits the jaws. It is wise to stabilize the weights when this is done.

The amount of weight you choose to use can vary. It must be enough to pull the web down snugly against the top of the cylinder but not enough to prevent the needles from rising. Some buckles slip and allow the weights to drop unexpectedly. Keep your feet and your pets out from under the weights. Having your left hand around your knitting while your right hand powers the machine may allow you to preserve your project if the buckle moves abruptly. If your buckle is consistently incompetent, you need to explore options of replacement or stabilization.

If practicing heels or after completing the toe of a sock (pouch structures), maintain your tension on the pouch and knit enough waste rows so that you will be able to move the buckle above the last pouch you have created. This lets you start your next practice element or next sock without having to worry about uneven pull on the web.

If you forget to move your buckle and the weight hits the floor, you will lose tension on your stitches and the web is likely to jump off the machine. If your weight hits an obstruction, like a horizontal support for your stand, you may lose your entire web or a section of it. As with a buckle that slips, having your left hand around your knitting while your right hand powers the machine may allow you to preserve your project when this happens.

# 7. STITCH SIZE OR TENSION ADJUSTMENTS

Each machine is capable of making a range of stitch sizes. This range may not be identical from one machine to another, even when comparing two machines that look like twins at first glance. Small changes in internal parts can have big effects on stitch range. Intentional design elements can also have a significant impact. The number of needles in use will also play a role. You need to become familiar with your machine's capabilities as this will affect your choice of yarns and the products you can make.

Beyond the mechanical parameters of an individual machine, each yarn has a range of stitch sizes specific to the yarn. Weight, twist, dye, and fiber content are all factors which can affect the size of stitches that can be made. Humidity is a factor which can cause short-term changes in a yarn's stitch range (drier fibers do not bend as easily, so the smaller stitches become more difficult).

The smallest stitch size an individual yarn can be knit without difficulty is identified as the standard tension for that yarn. Standard tension should be identified with the heel spring engaged for any project which requires the use of the heel spring. The heel spring has the effect of making the stitches smaller. Forcing the machine to knit a stitch smaller than the standard tension may damage the machine and stress the yarn. It is not a wise long-range strategy.

The gauge swatch exercise which follows will acquaint you with the range of stitch sizes your machine can make with a sample yarn. It will help you develop muscle memory for adjusting the stitch size. You will have practice adjusting the buckle and weights. You will work with one of the simple pattern stitches—the eyelet stitch. You should see and feel differences in operation and product as you move through the entire stitch range to help you understand some of the elements of the principles of size. If you knit two swatches and put one through any finishing process, you will be able to see the changes that must be considered once the item is removed from the machine. You may have the opportunity to restart your machine if something unexpected happens. You may also have to troubleshoot your system if your machine is not knitting well.

Although exaggerated in this exercise, a gauge swatch is a very helpful tool when attempting to create a sock of a specific size with an unfamiliar yarn. If you intend to determine the appropriate tension setting for a project, it is not usually necessary to sample the entire stitch range. As you gain experience, you will develop an understanding of the approximate setting and can fine tune it from that starting point.

# 8. GAUGE SWATCH

Begin your machine with waste yarn. When the tube is long enough to apply the buckle and have it hang independently, do so.

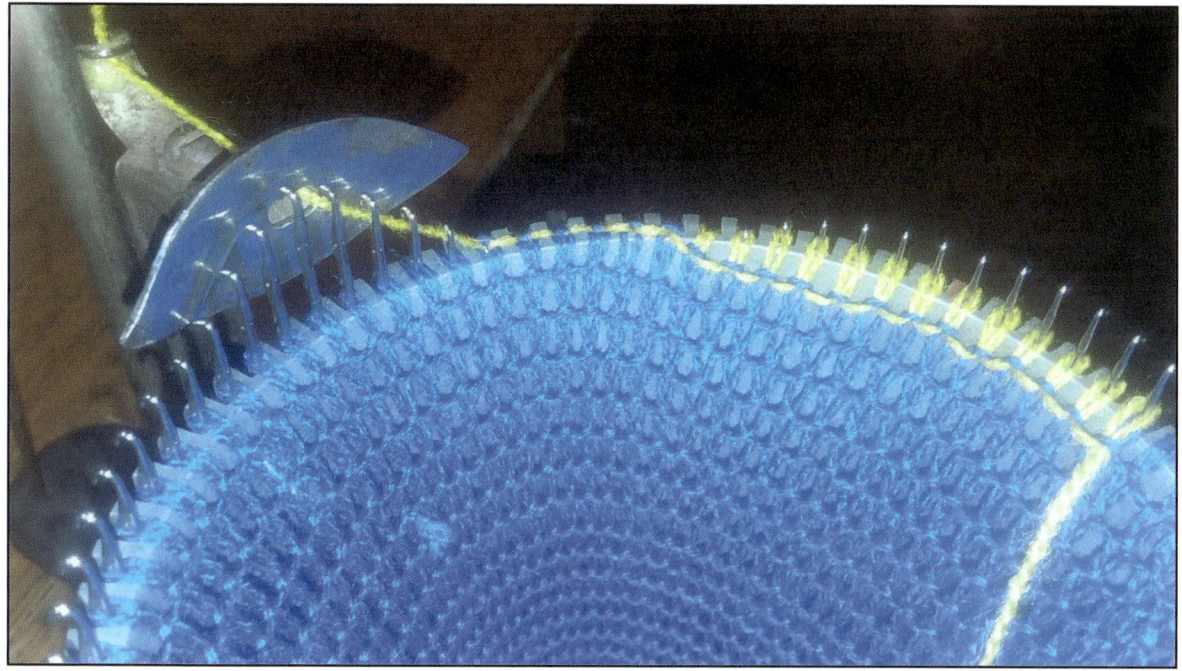

Adjust your machine to make the largest stitch possible without jamming the machine. Knit a few rows to test this setting. Stitches sometimes drop at low tension (large stitches) due to the character of the yarn. If this happens, first check to make sure your weight is pulling evenly on the web. If the weight is correct, reduce the stitch size in small increments until the stitches knit reliably. Switch to project yarn.

Knit the selvedge of your choice which does not require the ribber assembly. If you are not familiar with any selvedge technique, skip this selvedge step.

Knit 10 rows at this stitch size setting.

Engage the heel spring. Knit 10 rows. Note any difference between the size of original stitches and those created with the heel spring engaged. Continue to use the heel spring for the remainder of the exercise.

Advance the yarn carrier to the front of the machine, and set up an eyelet stitch behind (towards the back of the machine) the right half mark. The sequence will be right half mark, empty needle, two stitches on one needle, then all needles with a single stitch.

Knit another 10 rows at this stitch size setting. Stop the yarn carrier in the front of the machine.

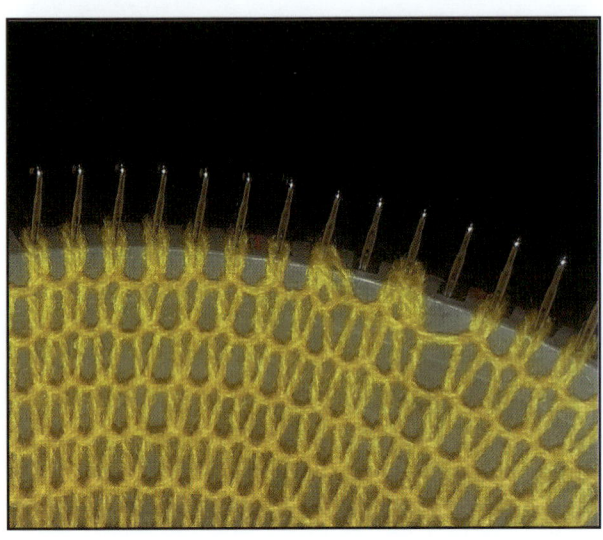

Set up two eyelet stitches, adjacent to each other, behind the right half mark. The sequence will be right half mark, empty needle, two stitches on one needle, empty needle, two stitches on one needle, then all needles with a single stitch. Remember that you are creating these eyelets in the knitting direction and they are being formed behind the right half mark—forward in terms of knitting and back in terms of the physical location on the cylinder.

Change the tension one setting, making your stitch size *SMALLER*. For this exercise, make one full revolution of your tension knob or nut. The direction of the turn will depend on the make and model of your machine.

Knit 10 rows at this stitch size setting. Stop the yarn carrier in the front of the machine.

Set up three eyelet stitches, adjacent to each other, behind the right half mark.

Change the tension one setting as before, continuing to make the stitch size *SMALLER*.

Knit 10 rows at this stitch size setting. Stop the yarn carrier in the front of the machine.

Continue this process of knitting 10 rows, making eyelet stitches (one additional eyelet stitch for each tension change), and reducing the stitch size, until the machine will no longer knit the stitches easily or until it reaches the outer limits of its stitch range (The nut or knob will no longer turn.)

This process may take many adjustments to cover the range of stitches possible.

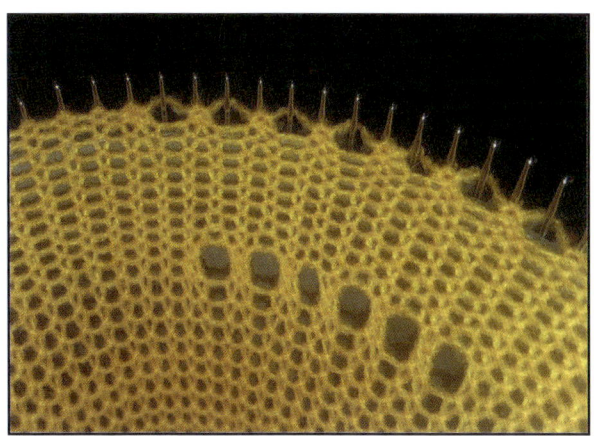

If the stitches do not settle back to the top of the cylinder when the needles are in the resting position, the tension is too high and the stitches are too small. Making the stitch slightly larger so that the web settles will adjust your setting to standard tension mentioned previously. This is the highest tension at which you should knit this particular yarn.

At the last setting which allows knitting, switch to waste yarn. Knit several rows. (It is important that the waste yarn be the same weight or finer than the yarn used for this exercise, or it will not knit at this tension setting.)

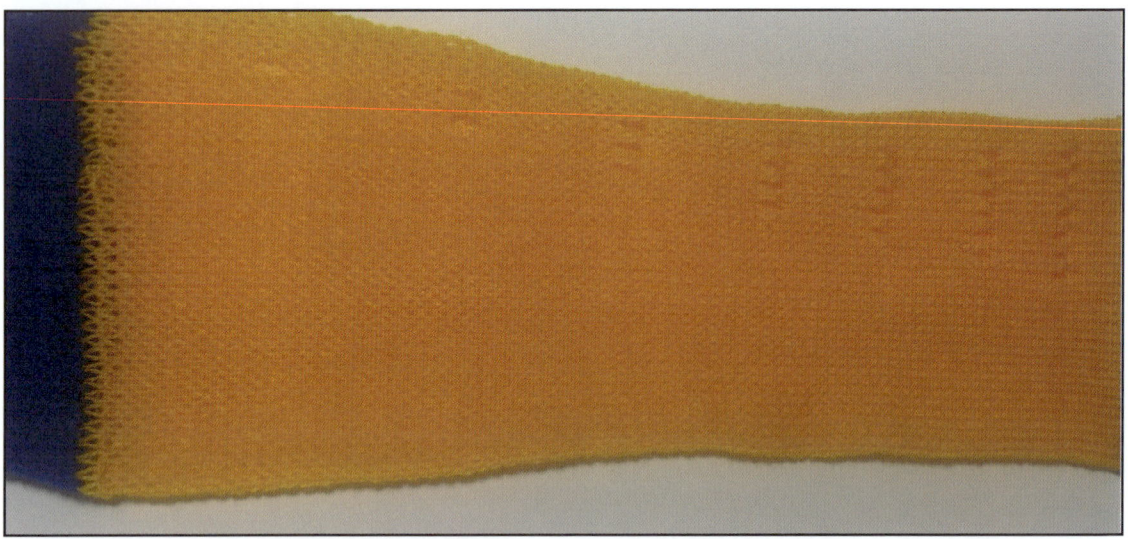

Remove the tube from the machine or begin another swatch project following the same procedure.

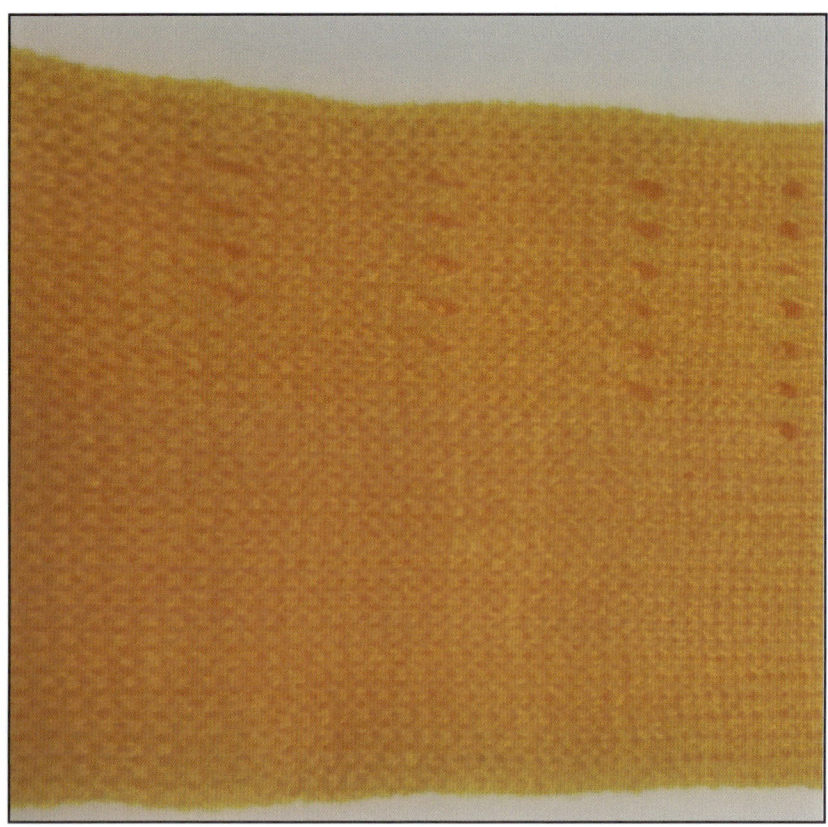

If you wish to save your swatch, the beginning edge is stable if you created a selvedge. The waste yarn can be removed without damaging the structure of the swatch. The final stitches will need to be stabilized. If you did not create a selvedge, both the beginning and the ending edges will require some sort of handwork to prevent them from running if the waste yarn is removed. A simple life line loop (a length of yarn threaded with a needle through each live stitch and secured without being drawn up or gathered) will be sufficient.

Measure the length of knitting between your single eyelet and your last successful setting when you remove the piece from the machine. Measure the same section again in 24 hours. In most cases, the length of the piece will be shorter after it rests. Many other measurements and observations can be useful, for example, the number of rows per inch of each interval (between each section of eyelet markers). These will change as the piece rests or if it is put through additional finishing (washing, drying, etc.).

It is useful to make one swatch that can be left as knit and a second that will be put through your chosen finishing process.

Remember to reposition the buckle and weights as necessary to keep tension on the web.

*Do not worry if you got distracted and lost count before changing settings, forgot an eyelet, made an extra eyelet, or somehow developed a run. It does not matter for this exercise. If your knitting drops off the machine or develops lots of runs or becomes snarled, start over and try again.*

# 9. SELVEDGES FOR THE BEGINNING

A knit selvedge is a self edge—a treatment of the edge of a garment that prevents stitches from working loose and being lost or creating runs. A run is a sequence of lost stitches which has developed in the same relative position throughout successive rows. Runs caused by dropped stitches (during the knitting process) move in a single direction in most circular knitting machine products. Runs caused by broken yarn can move in either direction.

Knit and purl stitches are both simple loops. They differ in the direction in which they are drawn through the stitch of the previous row. The integrity of the loop is created by connection with loops in successive courses. Without some method of anchoring, the first and last row of these structures will come undone with little provocation. Side seams with continuous yarn do not share this problem.

There are several anchoring methods that can be accomplished on the machine at the beginning of a project to create a selvedge. There are a few selvedge options for the end stitches. This material will cover the beginning options that require the machine to be involved. Methods which do not depend upon a ribber attachment will be discussed first followed by options possible with the use of the ribber.

The most simple method of creating a selvedge involves the tuck stitch. A tuck stitch is one in which a stitch remains on the needle (or is otherwise held out of work) but is bypassed and not knit for one or more rows and then is again knit. Knit or purl stitches with a tuck stitch on either side will be anchored and unable to run down into successive courses. On a circular knitting machine, a tuck stitch is usually accomplished by raising a needle out of work without removing the stitch it holds and then lowering it back into work position when the desired number of rows have been completed. For a tuck stitch selvedge, knit one row on all needles. Follow that with a row which alternates one knit stitch followed by one tuck stitch all the way around the cylinder. Return all raised needles to work and resume knitting. It appears that when this section is freed from the preceding waste yarn, the entire tuck row is generally lost as a large loop between the initial and third row, but the edge stitches will now be anchored. Some simple handwork may be necessary to adjust the final tension and/or remove the loop. While the tucked edge will provide a stable selvedge, some people do not like its ruffly appearance. This can be minimized by steaming the sock before removing waste or separator thread. It also becomes less noticeable on stockinette which rolls to hide the edge.

A second method of creating stable beginning stitches is to create a cross in the loop of the stitch before making the stitch for the next row. The old manuals describe a process called the E-wrap in which a tail of yarn is looped and crossed around each needle at the beginning of the knitting. A variant of this is to knit a row of stitches and then lift each off, twist it once to create a cross, and replace the stitch on its needle. All crosses should be made in the same direction—for example, the yarn coming into the stitch should always be cross to lie over the yarn exiting the stitch. A second variant is to pick up the float between each stitch and wrap it around one of the two adjacent needles, being consistent to either wrap all on the forward needle or all on the backward needle. This also has the effect of crossing the stitch. Any stitch which is not crossed will run.

A third method of creating a selvedge is to alternate knit and purl stitches on the second row of the edge (The first row is all knit; the second row is knit, purl.) This stitch sequence must be regular: no two knit stitches can lie next to each other; no two purl stitches can lie next to each other (There is an additional step which can override this sequence which will be discussed later.) After a stitch is knit, it can be manually converted to a purl stitch by removing it from the needle and reversing the direction in which the yarn passes through the loop from the previous course. Any error in converting knit to purl stitches which alters the sequence of knit, purl, knit, purl will result in a run. This edge has a bit of a ruffle which becomes less pronounced when the edge is stretched. At the top of a stockinette section, this selvedge will be hidden by the natural roll of the fabric edge as seen in the left end above. The right end has been pinned for visualization.

To create a knit stitch, insert a latch needle through a live stitch from the outside of the cylinder, catch the loose yarn, and pull it back to the outside of the cylinder. Loop that stitch over the needle. To create a purl stitch, insert a latch needle through a live stitch from the inside of the cylinder, catch the loose yarn, and pull it back to the inside of the cylinder. Loop that stitch over the needle. These are the same steps that are necessary if you are latching up a knit or purl stitch after a run on the machine.

A fourth method requires that the live beginning stitches OR the floats between each live beginning stitch be picked up, hung on needles and knit along with a later course of knitting. The choice must be consistent—either stitches or floats—for the entire length of the hem. This is typically called a hung hem. This process usually requires at least two rows of knitting past the beginning row before the pick-up process is initiated.

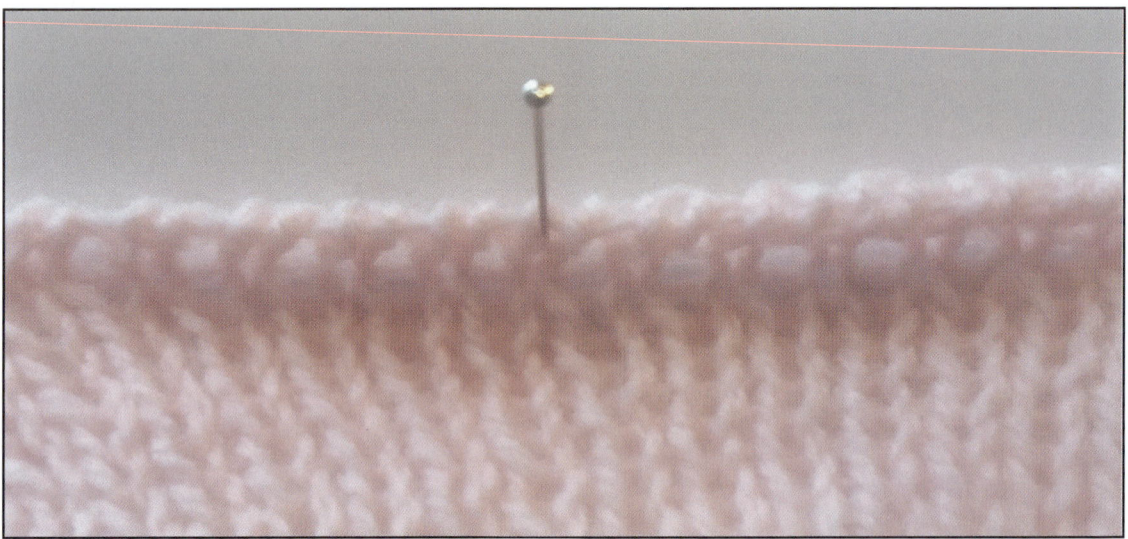

A few rows will create a thickened or rolled appearance.

Additional rows prior to pick-up will create a pocket (outside and inside views). A row of eyelet stitches knit in the center of of the hem rows will create a picot edge with multiple small peaks.

Every live stitch from the beginning row must be picked up and rehung on a needle or that stitch will run. More than one live stitch from that first row can be hung on the same needle without destabilizing the edge. The number of extra stitches a machine will be able to knit on a single needle will depend on the stitch size, yarn choice, and specific machine.

If a machine has a ribber attachment and a standard cylinder and dial combination (the cylinder having double the number of needle slots as the dial), the first row can be set as knit, purl, knit, purl and no other treatment is necessary. This is, of course, also possible with the new ribber dials which have the same number of slots as the cylinder, and may be an option with other combinations. The pitch of the sequence—aligned slots versus those which are offset—is not significant. The critical factor is that each knit stitch lie next to purl stitches and vice versa.

Some machines are sold with a ribber dial which did not have half the number of slots as the cylinder. While this was a common practice at one time, these are not what are typically called standard combinations. It is common to find an early Gearhart with a 24 slot ribber dial and a 72 slot cylinder. It is also common to find a Legare, Creelman, or Verdun machine with a 36 slot dial and a 54 slot cylinder. In both cases, it is not possible to set the machine to an every other stitch type pattern if all cylinder slots are to be used with a full pitch ribber. For these, an additional step must be taken to insure that the adjacent cylinder stitches do not run. That step is to pick up the float between the two cylinder stitches and wrap it around one of the two adjacent needles. As in an earlier method, this has the effect of crossing the stitch to prevent it from running. I have seen no reports of a similar method done on ribber needles if two purl stitches lie adjacent. Further experimentation may provide additional options.

# 10. BOTTLE / CAN / ICE CREAM SLEEVE

This project requires a selvedge, a tube, and a bit of hand work at the end. Many variations are possible. The use of the ribber attachments makes a sleeve which will fit most accurately, but a simple stockinette or mock rib sleeve is also useful.

Begin your machine with waste yarn. When the tube is long enough to apply the buckle and have it hang independently, do so.

Switch to project yarn.

Create the selvedge of your choice.

Knit enough rows to create a project yarn section of approximately four inches for an ice cream sleeve. You may want a slightly longer tube for a bottle, can, or all-purpose sleeve.

Leave a tail of several inches of unknit project yarn attached to the last stitch. Switch to waste yarn and knit several rows.

You can choose to continue knitting additional projects or remove the tube from the machine at this time.

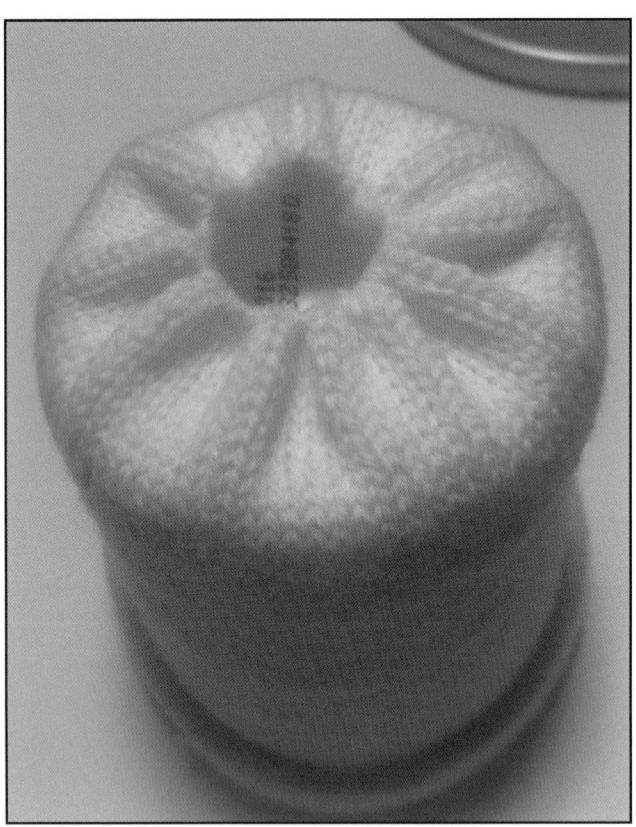

With the tube removed from the machine, thread the leftover unknit project yarn onto a needle. Guide the needle through each loop of the last row of the project yarn tube. Draw the yarn through as necessary to allow the needle movement. When the final stitch has been threaded, place the tube on a bottle, can, toe jack, or other object which can provide form. Draw the thread tight, gathering this final row of stitches until the opening in the center is about one inch across. Secure the end of the yarn and remove the excess.

If you close the end completely, the object you use the sleeve to cover may have difficulty sitting on a flat surface.

If your yarn is somewhat fragile, it may be desirable to make several rounds through the final row of stitches before tying off.

If your piece is too long for the object you wish to cover, simply fold the edge of the knit back on itself.

Remember to move the buckle and weights as necessary to keep tension on the web when knitting.

# 11. REVERSING AND SHORT ROW HEELS

The machine cannot reverse without dropping stitches unless needles are raised to the out of work position or removed from the machine. Most machines will also jam if these needles are not raised on a reverse. The minimum number of needles that must be moved or removed will depend on the design of the machine.

When changing direction, the machine should be cranked into the area of out of work (or missing) needles so that the trailing cam has fully cleared the in work section. It is good to develop the habit of taking the yarn carrier all the way to the back of the machine before reversing when knitting on needles in the front half of the machine, regardless of the make and model of the machine. This is a valuable practice even if the machine is capable of reversing more abruptly.

When setting the machine up for the heel process, the specific needle identified to be the first in work needle will depend upon your choice of pattern.

Most heel patterns work at least half the total number of stitches used for the ankle section of the sock. Increasing the number of needles used in a heel will create a deeper heel.

A short-row heel may be called by many names, among them the hourglass heel and the Niantic heel. This heel structure is created by working a series of rows which are decreased at the edges to a specific heel pivot point followed by a series of rows which are increased at the edges until all needles have been returned to work.

To decrease or narrow the heel, one needle is raised out of work with each pass of the yarn carrier (Patterns sometimes call for two needles to be raised on the first pass from each side but then revert to raising single needles thereafter.) The choice of needle alternates from side to side so that the decrease occurs evenly.

Raising the last needle to knit (rather than raising the last needle on the opposite side) reduces the likelihood of a dropped stitch. Tipping the raised needle out slightly will enlarge the last stitch just a little bit. This will make it easier to knit this stitch on the increase and reduce the appearance of small holes at the joint between the front and back halves of the heel. *Tip each needle after it is raised.*

A short row heel or toe is decreased until a specific number of needles are remaining in work in the center front of the machine.

To increase, the same process involving two needles on the first two passes and then one needle on each additional pass will be followed as with the decreases. However, instead of raising needles out of work and decreasing the number of worked stitches, needles will be lowered to return to work and the number of worked stitches will increase. This continues until all needles in the front half of the machine have been returned to work.

There are a number of methods for returning needles to work on the heel increase. One of these options will be covered shortly.

A toe may be knit following the same directions and process as this short row heel structure. The final edge of the toe will be grafted or otherwise secured to the final stitches of the foot after the knitting has been removed from the machine.

Some patterns, provided elsewhere, start the sock at the toe and work upwards to the welt above the leg section. The short row structure is the same regardless of the direction in which it is worked.

# 12. CYLINDER MARKINGS

Many old manuals contain diagrams for marking cylinders. The numerical choices vary slightly. Most are based on sections that are roughly 1/3 the total number of needles of the front half of the machine, *with equal portions for both right and left decreases*. If the number of needles does not divide cleanly into thirds, the extra needles can either lie on the decrease sides or central portion of the set up.

Gearhart illustrations divide cylinders as follows:
    60 total     30 half divided as 9/12/9
    72 total     36 half divided as 11/14/11
    80 total     40 half divided as 12/16/12
    100 total   50 half divided as 16/18/16

Auto Knitter illustrations divide cylinders as follows:
    60 total     30 half divided as 9/12/9
    80 total     40 half divided as 12/16/12
    100 total   50 half divided as 15/20/15

1/3 Rule of Thumb divides cylinders as follows:
    48 total     24 half divided as 8/8/8
    54 total     27 half divided as 9/9/9
    56 total     28 half divided as 9/10/9
    60 total     30 half divided as 10/10/10
    64 total     32 half divided as 10/12/10
    72 total     36 half divided as 12/12/12
    80 total     40 half divided as 13/14/13
    84 total     42 half divided as 14/14/14
    96 total     48 half divided as 16/16/16
    100 total   50 half divided as 16/18/16

Most knitters choose to mark the top edge of the cylinder at the half way points and in front of the last needle to be knit for the heel. Other important positions may also be identified.

Nail polish or automotive touch-up paint works well for this task. Marks can be easily removed with acetone when necessary. Typing correction fluid is sometimes used for short term or temporary project marks as it is easily removed and does not stain.

It is easiest if the markings are made so that the center front of the heel will correspond to the center of the cylinder as it sits in front of you, with the yarn mast slightly off to the left.

The original markings (the thinner red line on the cylinder edge below), were usually made as though the yarn mast was center back—a considerably less ergonomic position.

The heavier red mark shows the position of the half way point with the machine angle adjusted.

Some knitters choose to work heels and toes at the back of the machine and mark their cylinders accordingly. This is personal preference and does not alter the structure of the pieces.

Although many sock patterns knit the toe in the same shape as the heel, a second set of pivots can be marked if a different toe shaping is desired.

# 13. WEIGHTING THE HEEL

The need for weight on the stitches as the machine knits has already been established. The buckle system pulls on the entire web. If a section of needles is worked while others remain idle, the resulting stitches will need additional weight. The V-hook (heel hook) was provided as standard equipment with most machines to accomplish this task. This dual hook system can be used regardless of whether the ribber attachment is on or off the machine.

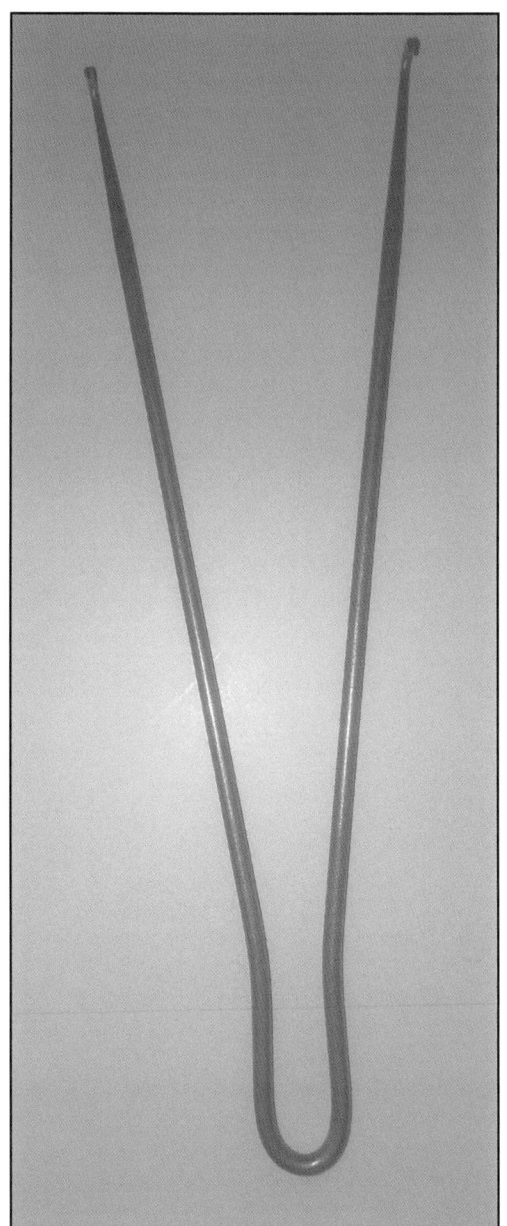

A heel hook can be a one piece unit or two separate pieces joined by a cord or wire. The one piece units are typically a rod or wire bent to a V or U shape with each terminal end curved into a hook. The two piece units are rods or wires with hooks at one end and an eye or slot at the other. These pieces are joined with a cord or wire (through the eye or slot) for this particular application. These two hooks sometimes have a latch or tongue near the hook. The hooks pierce the web and hang with the tips inside the knitting and the stems between the knitting and the inside cylinder wall. Weight is hung from the center of the V or from the cord between the pieces so that pull is exerted on each hook at the same time.

When it is time to knit a heel decrease, needles at the back half of the machine will be raised out of work and the yarn carrier will be resting at the back of the machine. Before making the first reverse pass, hang the heel hook in the web. It is very difficult to get clear photographs of placement for the heel hook. Many of the original vintage manuals have drawings which provide more information.

Place each hook about six rows below the edge of the cylinder and six stitches towards the center from each of the outermost needles which will be knitting. It is not necessary for this to be exact, and successful placement usually takes trial and error and practice. Try to get both hooks to hang in spaces in the same row so that the pull will be even.

Hang a stem weight from the center of the V or the connecting cord. If necessary, this weight can be shifted from the buckle to do this duty; but you must remember that you no longer have weights on half the web. It is better to have an additional weight for the heel hook device and leave your primary weight stack in place. Weights between a half pound and a pound should be sufficient for the heel hook. As you are knitting your reverses, your left hand should be on this hook and weight arrangement. That will allow you to manually increase the downward pull if necessary. You will also learn to feel dropped stitches from this position.

The heel hook is exerting most of its pull on the outermost stitches of the heel—the edges where the decreases are taking place. These stitches are more likely to rise and drop off improperly during this process than those in the very center of the machine. This critical area shifts inward towards the center front with each pass as needles are raised out of work. For this reason, the heel hook must be repositioned every several rows. With each position change, apply the same general rule of thumb—six rows from the top of the cylinder and six stitches in from the outermost knitting needles. Continue making adjustments until the decreases have reached the pivot points of the heel.

For the second half of the heel, some people leave the heel hook in the center position it achieved at the end of the decrease and merely move it upward every few rows of the increase. Others prefer to reverse the original process and follow the expansion with about six rows and six stitches between the insertion point and the outermost needles as they now increase. Find a process that works well for you. It does not have to be one that meets the needs or expectations of anyone else.

Single piece V-hooks are generally somewhat springy so that they can be flexed to accommodate a variety of positions. A few are heavier and less willing to bend. These will occasionally snap during use. Treat them gently to get them to last as long as possible. Beware of the hooks of these single piece units. They are frequently extremely sharp.

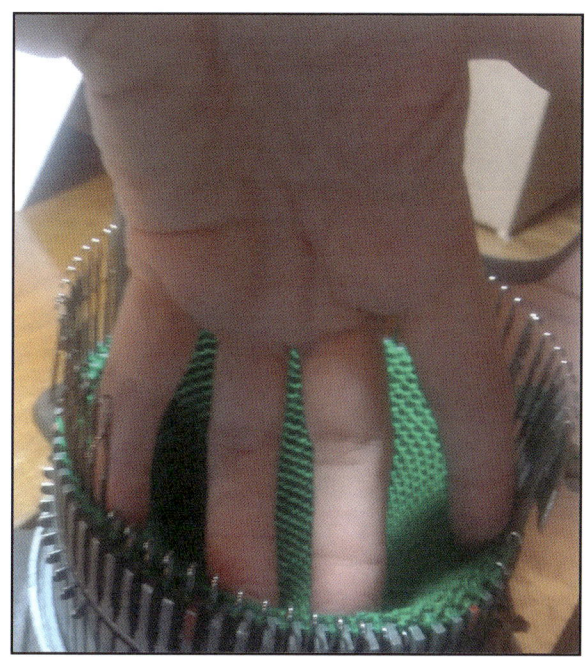

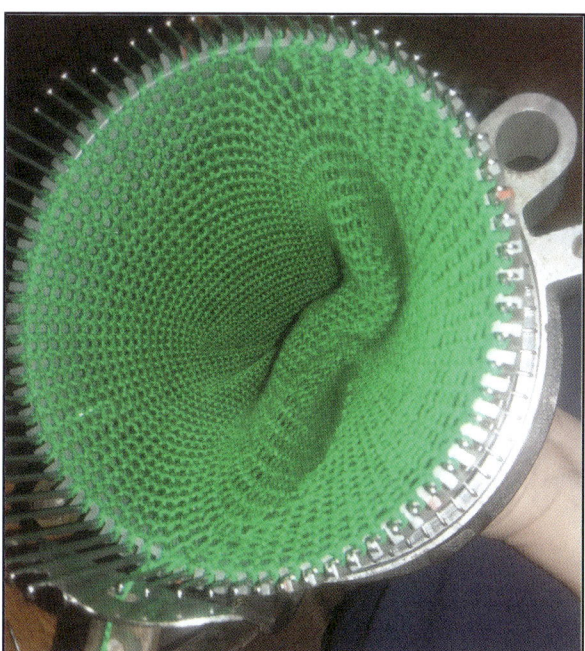

It should be noted that the entire heel can be knit without a special accessory if the left hand is used to pull or push down on the web during the knitting pass. This can be done from the top edge of the machine with a splayed or fanned hand with the palm facing outward if there is no ribber on the machine or from the underside of the machine with the section of knitting being pulled down by a pinch process.

55

# 14. SHORT ROW HEEL WITH WRAP ON THE INCREASE

Read all the way through these instructions and the heel tips included before you attempt to knit your first heel. Before you begin knitting, make sure your cylinder markings are visible and your needle counts are correct.

PRE-HEEL

Knit at least 10 rows of stockinette, counting at the right half mark.

After the 10$^{th}$ row, knit forward until the yarn carrier is at the front of the machine.

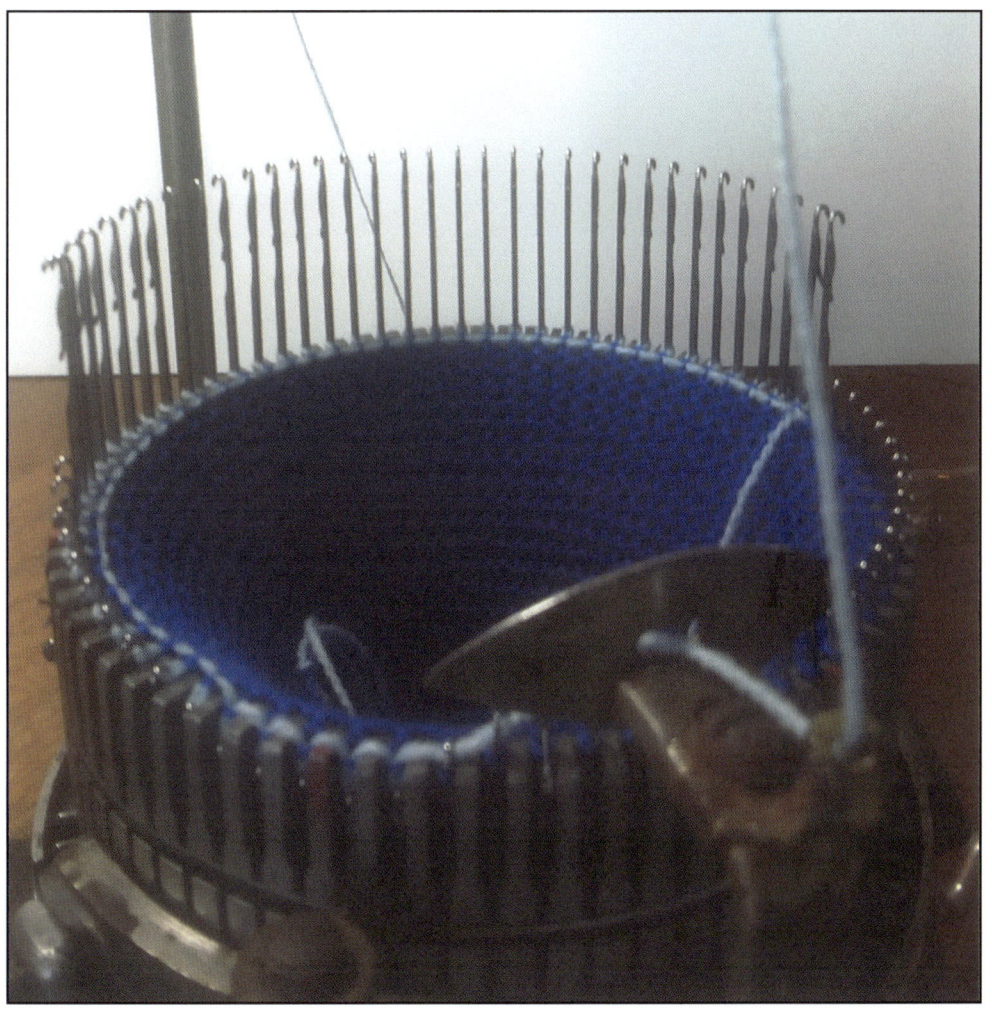

# HEEL

Raise all the needles in the back half of the cylinder except the two that are next to the right and left half marks (one needle on the left and one on the right for a total of two needles). Do this by starting at the right half mark. Skip the first needle behind the mark. It will stay in work. Raise the next needle, and continue around the back of the cylinder raising needles until you reach the last needle behind (to the back of the machine) the left half mark. This needle will stay in work. You should now have:

      22 needles raised out of work on a 48 slot cylinder
      25 needles raised out of work on a 54 slot cylinder
      28 needles raised out of work on a 60 slot cylinder
      30 needles raised out of work on a 64 slot cylinder
      34 needles raised out of work on a 72 slot cylinder
      38 needles raised out of work on an 80 slot cylinder
      40 needles raised out of work on an 84 slot cylinder
      46 needles raised out of work on a 96 slot cylinder
      48 needles raised out of work on a 100 slot cylinder

Engage the heel spring. For most common Y-style tops, pick up the yarn between the yarn stand top brake and the front hole or fork of the top, and loop it over the hook of the heel spring. For less common designs, refer to the machine manual for threading information.

Check to make sure that the brake pinches the yarn against some element of the mast top. If it does not, you have probably looped the wrong portion of the yarn through the heel spring. If the brake should be making contact but is not, it may need to be adjusted (bent).

When the machine is reversed, the heel spring is necessary to take up the yarn drawn out when the carrier was moved to the back of the machine.

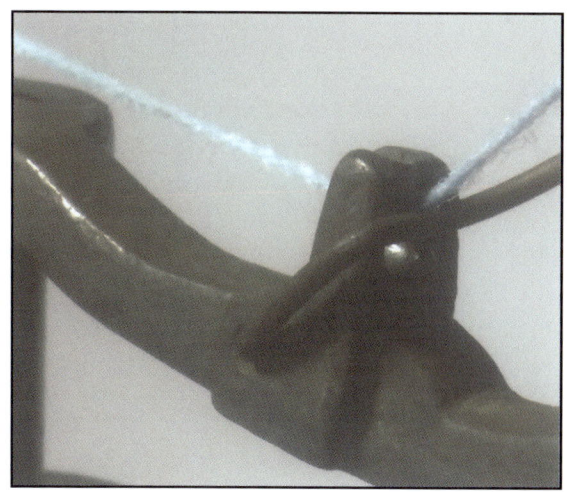

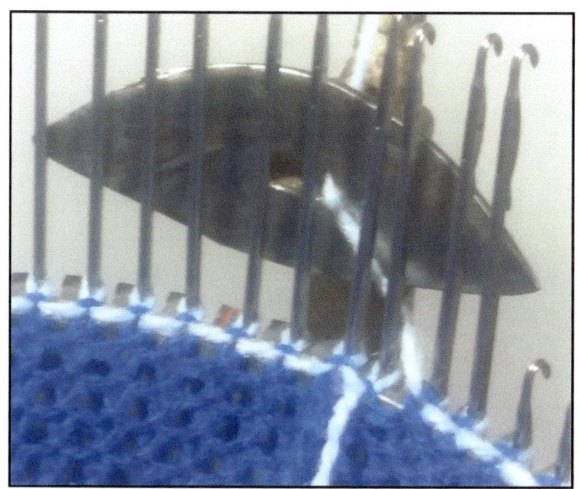

If the heel spring is working correctly, as the carrier reaches the in work needles, there will be minimal slack.

If the heel spring is not working correctly, the yarn will be slack and may have loops. If this excess yarn is not pulled up by the heel spring or manually, there may be extra loops in the heel or stitches may drop at the heel edge.

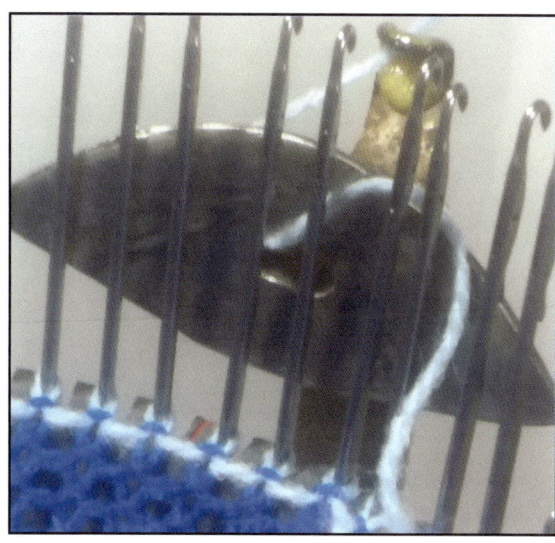

## DECREASE (first half of the heel)

**Note** the back and forth process on one section of needles will create slack in the tension of the web—in this case, the web at the front of the machine. You will need to add downward pull with your hand or one of the tensioning devices (heel hold down, V-hook, heel forks, etc.) to keep the stitches from rising on the needles. On some machines, and at some tensions, you will need to start this hold down right away. On other machines, and at other tensions, you may be able to knit several rows before you are aware of the slack. Develop the habit of adding the tension right away to avoid mishaps. You should usually maintain some level of tension in this area until you are able to move your buckle up over this part of your web.

Knit forward until the yarn carrier is at the center back of the machine.

60

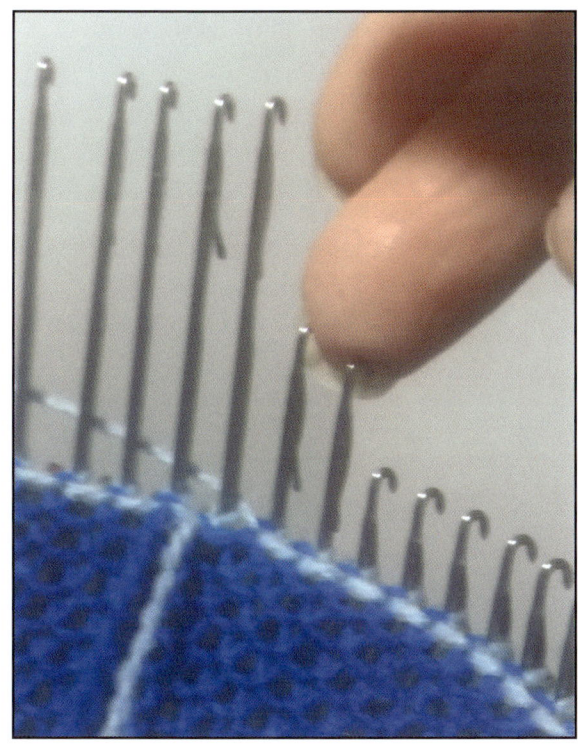 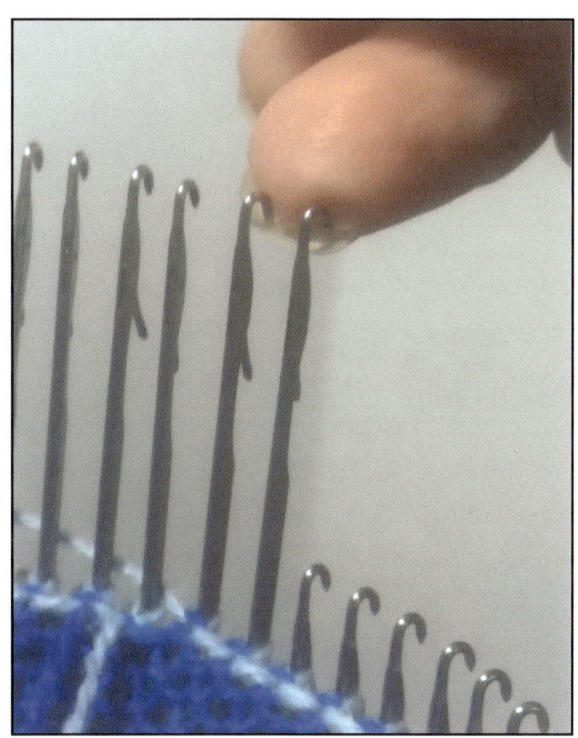

Raise the first two needles out of work on the right side of the machine. One will be on either side of the half mark.

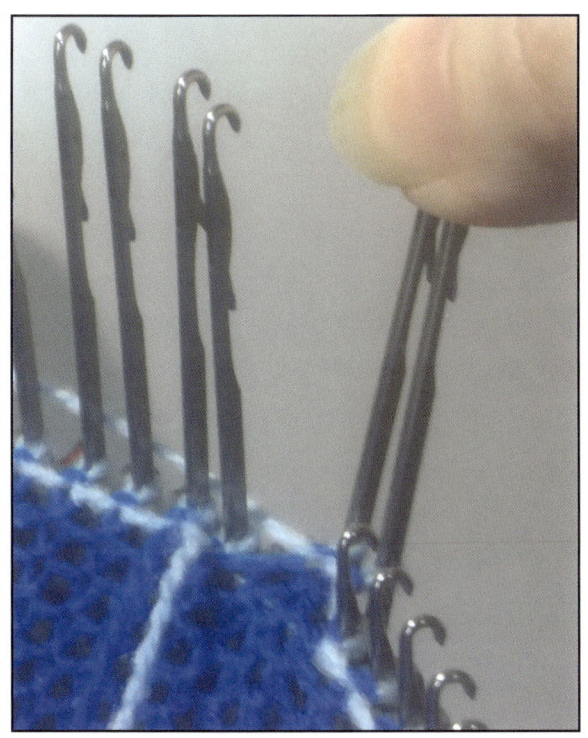

Tip the needles outwards to increase the stitch size slightly. This will help balance a heel spring which pulls aggressively and will minimize holes at the diagonal joins of the front and back half of the heel.

Reverse direction, and knit to the left across the front of the machine past all of the in work needles. Continue until the yarn carrier is at the center back of the machine.

Raise the first two needles out of work on the left side of the machine. One will be on either side of the half mark.

**Two needles are raised on each side in this manner at the start of the heel to minimize a significant hole which develops as this structure begins. Single needles are raised on all the remaining passes.

Reverse direction and knit to the right across the front of the machine and on until the yarn carrier is at the back.

Raise the first in work needle on the right side of the machine to the out of work position.

Reverse direction and knit to the left across the front of the machine and on until the yarn carrier is at the back.

Raise the first in work needle on the left side of the machine to the out of work position.

Continue this back and forth process, raising one needle with each pass, until you reach the front heel marks.

** The number of needles that will remain in work at this point will vary depending on the number of needles in the cylinder and the source followed for cylinder marking.

Once you have raised the final needle on the left side, make one more knitting pass across the front and stop the yarn carrier at the back of the machine. You have finished the decrease and are ready to begin the increase.

## INCREASE (second half of the heel)

Lower the first two needles on the right side of the cylinder.

** At this point, the yarn between the last stitch you have just knit and the yarn carrier will be lying in front of the newly lowered needles.

Pick up the yarn and guide it behind both of those needles and back out in front of the out of work needles beyond. Make sure the latches of all in work needles are open.

** Now, the yarn will be coming from the last stitch you have just knit, behind both newly lowered needles, back in front of the out of work needles, and on around to the yarn carrier. This action of moving the yarn behind the needles is the wrap process.

Knit to the left across the front of the machine and on until the yarn carrier is at the back.

Lower the first two out of work needles on the left side of the cylinder.

Pick up the yarn and guide it behind both of the newly lowered needles and back out in front of the out of work needles beyond. Make sure the latches are open.

** Again, the yarn will be coming from the last stitch you have just knit, behind both newly lowered needles, back in front of the out of work needles, and on around to the yarn carrier.

Reverse directions and knit to the right across the front of the machine and on until the yarn carrier is at the back.

Lower the first out of work needle on the right side of the cylinder.

Pick up the yarn and guide it behind this newly lowered needle. Check the latch.

Reverse directions and knit to the left across the front of the machine and on until the yarn carrier is at the back.

Lower the first out of work needle on the left side of the cylinder.

Pick up the yarn and guide it behind this newly lowered needle. Check the latch.

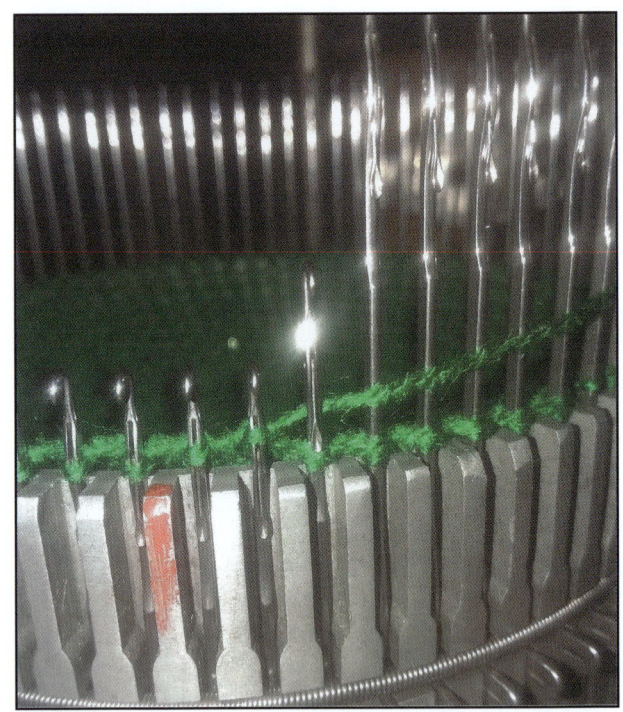

Reverse directions and knit to the right across the front of the machine and on until the yarn carrier is at the back.

Continue this back and forth process, lowering one needle per side until you have reached the needle in front of the half mark on the LEFT. This should be the only needle that is still raised in front of either half mark, and is the last needle to return to work to complete the increase. Wrap as usual.

Reverse directions and knit to the front of the machine. Stop with the yarn carrier in the front.

On this pass, you will have completed the heel when you reach the right half mark. You will be continuing with the body of the sock without the heel spring. It is now time to lower the back needles. Place them back down into the work position. Check to make sure all the latches are open.

Knit forward to the right half mark and take the yarn out of the heel spring. This is your zero point for counting rows in your sock foot.

# TIPS

You can raise the needles out of work with your fingers, a pick-up tool or hook, with a heel crescent, or with other unique tools. On some machines, you may have the option of using a heel lifter device built into the cam shell. The heel crescent and heel lifter device both allow several needles to be lifted at once. This improves speed during this stage of the process. However, manually lifting each needle allows you to feel the position of each needle and provides a counting opportunity to act as a double check to insure that you have the desired needles out of work.

The needle hooks are sharp. Be aware of this if you choose to use your fingers to raise the needles.

Raise the needles until the butts hit the cylinder spring. Throughout the heel process, the butts must stay up by this spring while out of work. If a butt drops down, it is likely to interfere with the V-cam and cause a jam. If the machine jams or hesitates (feels like it has hit an obstruction and then clears), look to see if the out of work needles have drooped a bit. The needle may have dropped far enough to be an obvious obstruction. The cause of a hesitation may be a little harder to identify. A butt may drop down a little way, get hit by the V-cam to cause a slight hitch, but then move back up out of the way. It is easy to knock the raised needles down a little with your arm or part of your clothing. They may also sag a bit if the cylinder spring is loose or damaged. If you have ongoing problems with this, you may need to add an extra check to make sure the needles have remained up prior to each pass of the yarn carrier, or you may need to shorten or replace your cylinder spring.

When you thread your heel spring, if you have picked up the yarn in the right place, the brake will pinch the yarn when you draw back on the source end (the end coming from the cone or bobbin). If the brake does not pinch the yarn, check to make sure you have picked up the right section of yarn for the heel spring loop (Check your threading drawing if necessary.) If you are sure you have the heel spring threading correct, the brake may be misaligned or damaged.

The position of the first working needles at the corners of the heels varies from one set of instructions to another. This variance affects the shape and size of the heel, and may be adjusted within a pattern for a specialized fit. The farther back on the cylinder that the heel process begins (when knitting the heel at the front of the machine), the wider the heel at the top, and the deeper the heel cup. The farther forward the heel begins, the narrower the top of the heel, and the more shallow the heel cup. Heels that tend to scootch down under your foot as you walk are usually the result of a short sock foot and/or a heel cup that is too shallow for your heel. If you have tried increasing the length of your socks and are still having your heels migrate during wear, consider altering your pattern to create a deeper heel cup. For instance, leave two needles in work behind the half mark on each side when setting up for the decrease.

To be able to keep track of where you are in the heel process:
    **On the decrease, the needle to be raised out of work will be the last one you have just knit. It is the last in work needle on the side with the yarn coming from the carrier. If you need to, follow the yarn with your eyes back from the carrier to identify this needle. This is sometimes referred to as the yarn carrier side even though you have actually stopped the carrier at center back.
    **On the increase, the needle to be returned to work will be next to the last one you have just knit. It is the first out of work needle on the side with the yarn coming from the carrier. The yarn to the carrier will be coming from the last stitch knit.

The last stitch you knit in any pass gets an extra tug from the action of the heel spring. This usually makes the corner stitch a little tighter than desired. This extra tension can make the stitch difficult to knit and can also exaggerate holes at the diagonal join of the heel. To counteract this yarn rob back, tip the hook end of the needle outward slightly when the needle is raised to the out of work position on the decrease or after returning to the work position for the increase. You will see that this makes the stitch a little larger again.

Lower needles back into the work position firmly but without excessive force. If you pop the needles back into work without care, the needle latches often hit the stitches and bounces up to close the needles. This can cause dropped stitches or time wasted opening latches. With most machines, leaving the needle slightly raised as it is put back into work will reduce the likelihood of a closed latch. The Legare machines generally work better with the needles returned to a fully engaged level, however.

Knit the toe as the heel. After the final pass of the toe, you will either change to waste yarn and pull a tail of sock yarn into the cylinder or you will knit several more rows with your sock yarn on all needles to be unraveled later. Either the tail or the extra rows provides the yarn for your toe closure.

# 15. DRAWSTRING PURSE OR MARBLE BAG

This project requires a selvedge, a tube, a ribbon or cord, and a bit of hand work at the end. The cord can be created on the machine if desired. Many variations are possible.

Begin your machine with waste yarn. When the tube is long enough to apply the buckle and have it hang independently, do so.

Switch to project yarn.

Create the selvedge of your choice. A hung hem is very nice for this project.

Knit approximately two rows.

Create a row of eyelet stitches by transferring every other stitch to an adjacent needle and leaving the empty needles in the machine to begin knitting on the next row. (The transfer must be done in at least two stages because it is not possible to reach all stitches at once.)

Knit enough rows to create a project yarn section of approximately six inches. This depth can be varied.

Knit a short row heel. Weight it appropriately.

Leave a tail of several inches of unknit project yarn attached to the project. Switch to waste yarn and knit several rows.

You can choose to continue knitting additional projects or remove the tube from the machine at this time.

With the project removed from the machine, thread the leftover unknit project yarn onto a needle. Kitchener (graft) the seam. For the method shown, the waste yarn is removed as it is replaced by the project yarn, providing a visual guide for the yarn path.

Secure the end of the yarn and remove the excess.

Thread a length of ribbon or cord through the eyelets formed by the picot stitch and tie the ends together to form a drawstring. (If there are an uneven number of eyelets, skip one.)

Remember to move the buckle and weights as necessary to keep tension on the web.

# 16. CORD

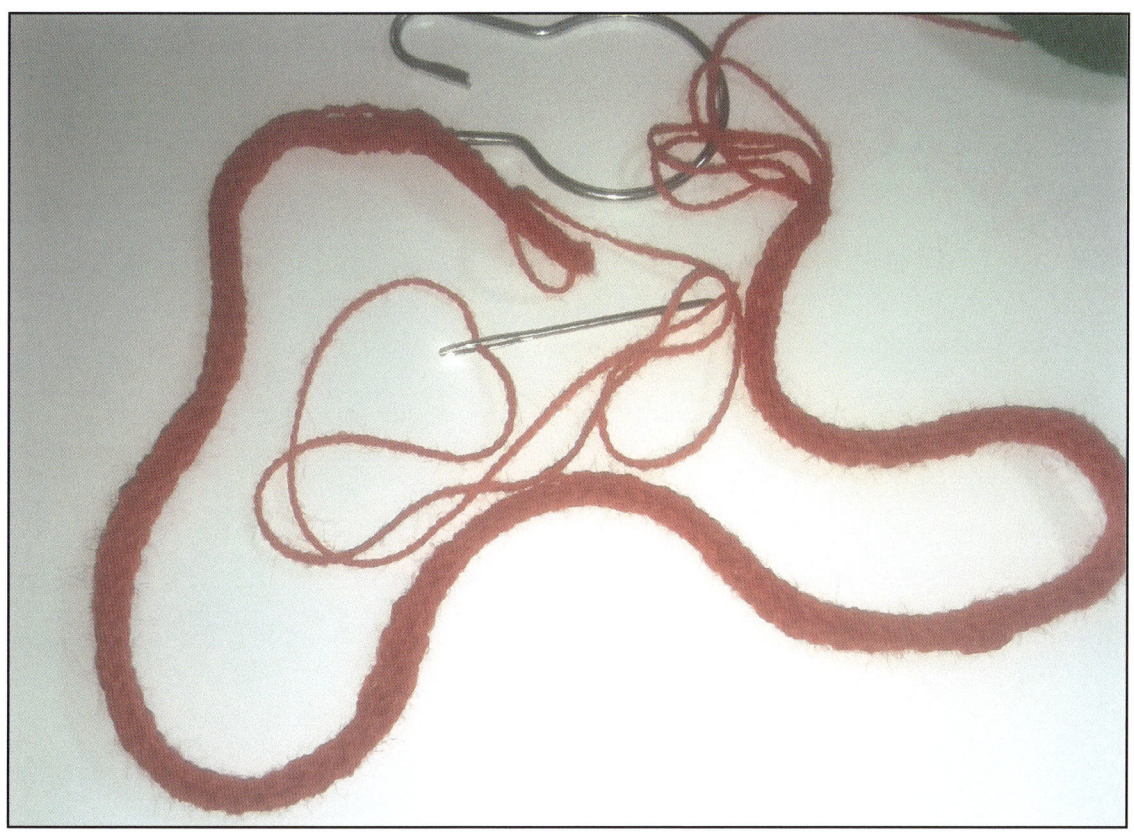

This project is a tubular structure worked on a small number of cylinder needles with the heel spring engaged. A little bit of hand work will be necessary to secure the ends of the cord.

Remove all cylinder needles except for four in a row at the front of the machine.

Use the set up bonnet or similar device to create a loop on each of these needles. You will pull down on the bonnet or device to provide tension during the early rows.

Begin with project yarn. Make one pass to establish knitting.

Engage your heel spring.

Continue knitting forward, past all the empty needle slots, until you make a second row, knitting in the forward direction. The yarn carrier will travel all the way around the cylinder.

Knit additional rows in this manner to the desired length of cord, maintaining downward pull on the stitches throughout the process.

Finish knitting the cord with a length of waste yarn or by running the project off the machine.

Remove the waste yarn. Cord ends will have live stitches. Thread the project yarn through a needle and catch each live end stitch, securing the end to prevent unraveling.

The number of stitches chosen will affect the shape of the cord. Even numbered stitches will make a cord which tends to flatten easily. Odd numbered stitches make a cord which will retain a more cylindrical shape. The weight of the yarn and size of the stitches will affect this appearance.

The width of the row will determine the maximum number of needles that can be used for a solid cord. The yarn float created between the back of the first and last needle in the row will become exaggerated as the width of knitting increases.

As with other knitting, the needles require tension on the previous stitches to form new stitches correctly. The cord involves so few needles that a buckle and normal weight is overwhelming. Tension can be provided by hand or with a significantly smaller weight.

# 17. TUCK STITCH TOP STOCKINETTE SOCK

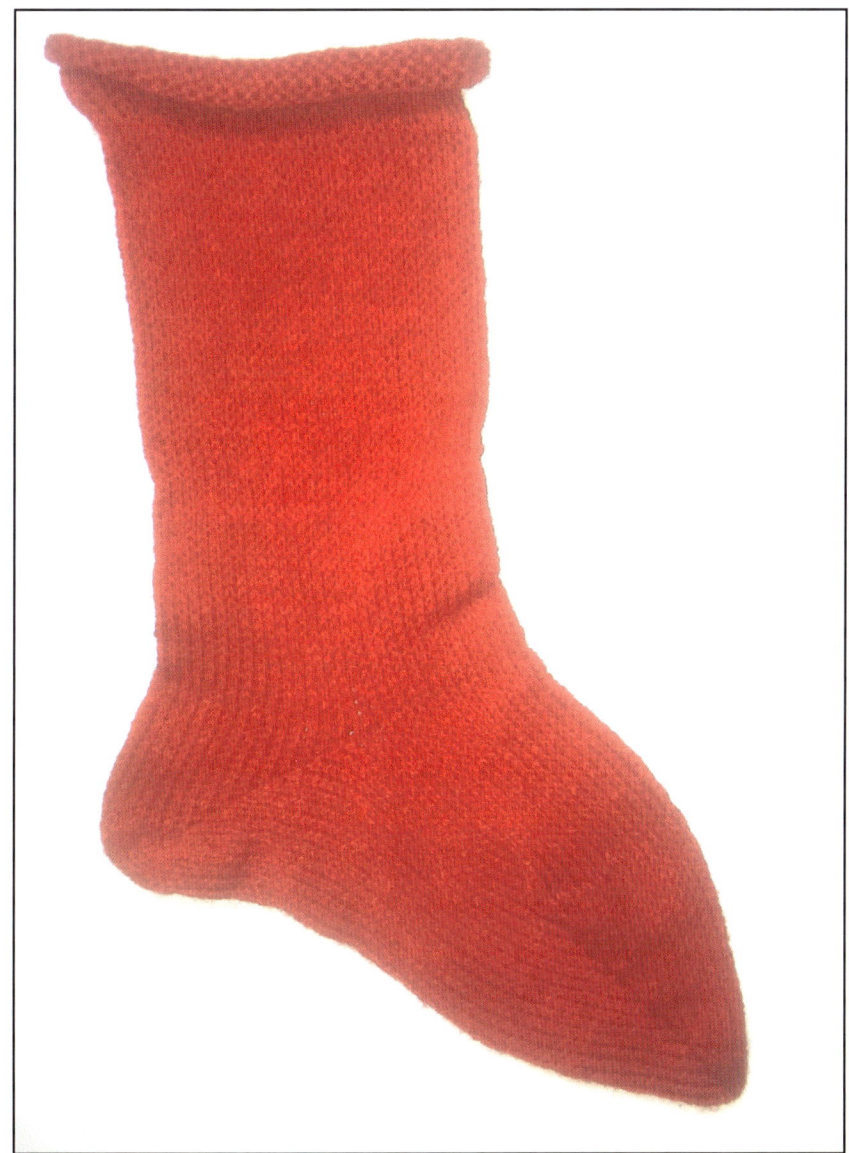

Cast on with waste yarn and knit at least 10 rows (Knit enough rows so that the buckle and weights are in use before beginning the sock.)

Change to sock yarn (right half mark).

Knit one row (count at right half mark). Begin a second row and stop the yarn carrier at the front of the machine.

Tuck stitch row—starting in front of the right half mark (in the knitting direction, towards the back of the machine) raise every other needle in sequence as far as the machine allows. When you reach a section of needles that cannot be raised near the trailing edge of the tension cam, knit forward ¼ to ½ row and continue the needle raising process. When the yarn carrier reaches the center front of the machine, lower the raised needles which can be moved easily, beginning at the right half mark and working in the knitting direction. Advance the machine, knitting another portion of this row, and then lower the raised needles that have been bypassed. Eventually all needles will be lowered on this second row.

*\*\*Note: If you come around to the half mark in the row for which you are raising needles and you find that two needles will be raised side-by-side, you have made an error in the sequence somewhere. At this point, you will need to begin the project again. Add another section of waste yarn and make another attempt.*

Knit 60 rows. (This is the leg from the top of the heel to the selvedge at the top of the sock.) Sock leg length can be varied according to taste or style.

Apply the heel spring and knit 10 rows of pre-heel.

Knit the heel.

Remove the heel spring and knit 40 rows for the body of the sock. (Foot length can be varied according to taste or style. Tension and yarn choices will affect the number of rows required. The heel and toe stitches will usually account for approximately 3 ½ to 4 inches.)

Knit the toe.

Join waste yarn to the project yarn, leaving at least two feet of project yarn attached for grafting. Pull this tail through to the inside of the tube, and knit waste on all cylinder needles for several rows before beginning the next sock or removing the project from the machine.

Close the toe after removing the sock from the machine.

When the waste yarn is removed from the tuck stitch selvedge, you may encounter a loop of yarn created by this technique. It can be worked back into the sock, tied off, or broken and woven in as you choose.

Stockinette rolls, so the tuck stitch top will be hidden in many projects.

# 18. TUCK STITCH TOP MOCK RIBBED SOCK

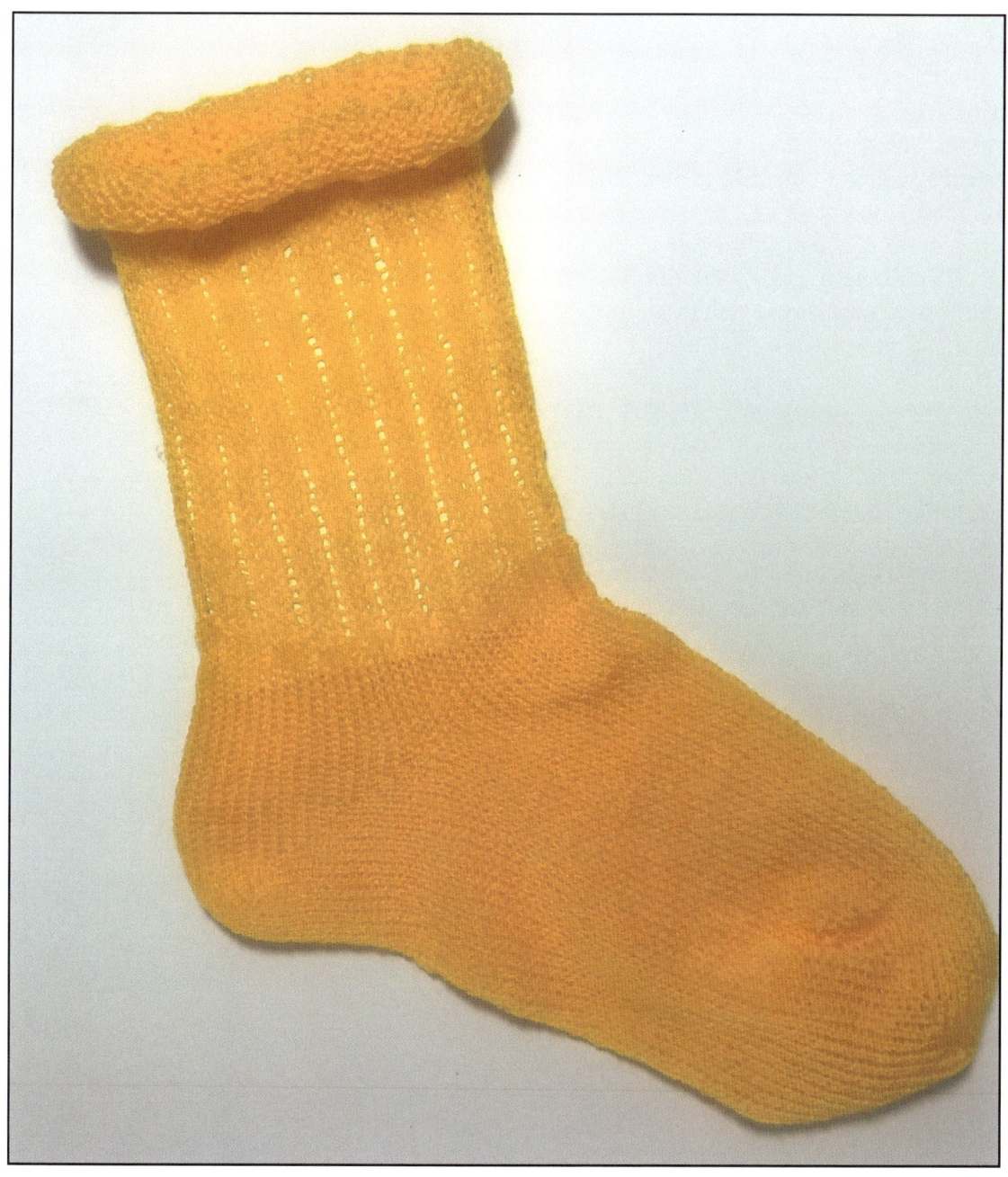

Remove every 4$^{th}$ needle from the machine if the cylinder count can be evenly divided by four (48, 56, 60, 64, 72, 80, 84, 96, 100). Remove every 3$^{rd}$ needle from the machine if the cylinder cannot be evenly divided by four (54).

Cast on with waste yarn and knit at least 10 rows (Knit enough rows so that the buckle and weights are in use before beginning the sock.)

Change to sock yarn (right half mark).

Knit one row (count at right half mark). Begin a second row and stop the yarn carrier at the front of the machine.

Tuck stitch row—starting in front of the right half mark (in the knitting direction, towards the back of the machine) raise every other needle in sequence as far as the machine allows. When you reach a section of needles that cannot be raised near the trailing edge of the tension cam, knit forward ¼ to ½ row and continue the needle raising process. When the yarn carrier reaches the center front of the machine, lower the raised needles which can be moved easily, beginning at the right half mark and working in the knitting direction. Advance the machine, knitting another portion of this row, and then lower the raised needles that have been bypassed. Eventually all needles will be lowered on this second row.

**Note: If you come around to the half mark in the row for which you are raising needles and you find that two needles will be raised side-by-side, you have made an error in the sequence somewhere. At this point, you will need to begin the project again. Add another section of waste yarn and make another attempt.*

Knit 60 rows. (This is the leg from the top of the heel to the selvedge at the top of the sock.) Sock leg length can be varied according to taste or style.

Replace the needles removed in the first step and put them in the work position. Go as far as you can without moving the yarn carrier and then stop.

Each needle preceding an empty needle has a live stitch hanging and an old stitch below that (the stitch from the previous row). Starting at the right half mark, pick up each old stitch and hang it over each adjacent empty needle, always moving the stitches in the knitting direction.

Move the yarn carrier as necessary to complete this process of adding needles and hanging stitches until all needle slots are filled.

Knit one complete row. Every needle should now be knitting.

Apply the heel spring and knit 10 rows of pre-heel.

Knit the heel.

Remove the heel spring and knit 40 rows for the body of the sock. (Foot length can be varied according to taste or style. Tension and yarn choices will affect the number of rows required. The heel and toe stitches will usually account for approximately 3 ½ to 4 inches.)

Knit the toe.

Join waste yarn to the project yarn, leaving at least two feet of project yarn attached for grafting. Pull this tail through to the inside of the tube, and knit waste on all cylinder needles for several rows before beginning the next sock or removing the project from the machine.

Close the toe after removing the sock from the machine.

When the waste yarn is removed from the tuck stitch selvedge, you may encounter a loop of yarn created by this technique. It can be worked back into the sock, tied off, or broken and woven in as you choose.

The step of hanging stitches from the previous row when needles are added to the machine can be omitted by choice. Needles can be added in sequence and should pick up loops on the first knitting pass, then begin to form true stitches on the second pass. If this option is followed, there will be a slight hole where the knitting begins for each replaced needle. This is not a flaw. It is a design element based on a choice of techniques.

If stitches are hung on the replaced needles, the latches for those needles are most likely to be open, and new stitches should form. If stitches are not hung on these needles, the machine should make a loop around the empty needle on the first pass and begin knitting true stitches on the second. The latch may not be open and should be checked. Some machines are better at forming loops on empty needles than others. If your machine is not consistently forming the loop on the first pass, leave the empty needle raised for one row after it is returned to the machine. Lower the needle before the second row begins. This should establish a loop on the first row and the stitch on the second.

The pre-heel is the ankle area. This process adds the needles before the pre-heel for a solid section of knitting above the heel. An alternative is to add the needles after the pre-heel so that the mock ribs run all the way to the foot. It is unusual to continue mock ribs into the heel, but they may be continued down the length of the top or sides of the foot as desired.

Stockinette rolls, so the tuck stitch top will be hidden in many projects.

# 19. HUNG HEM TOP STOCKINETTE SOCK

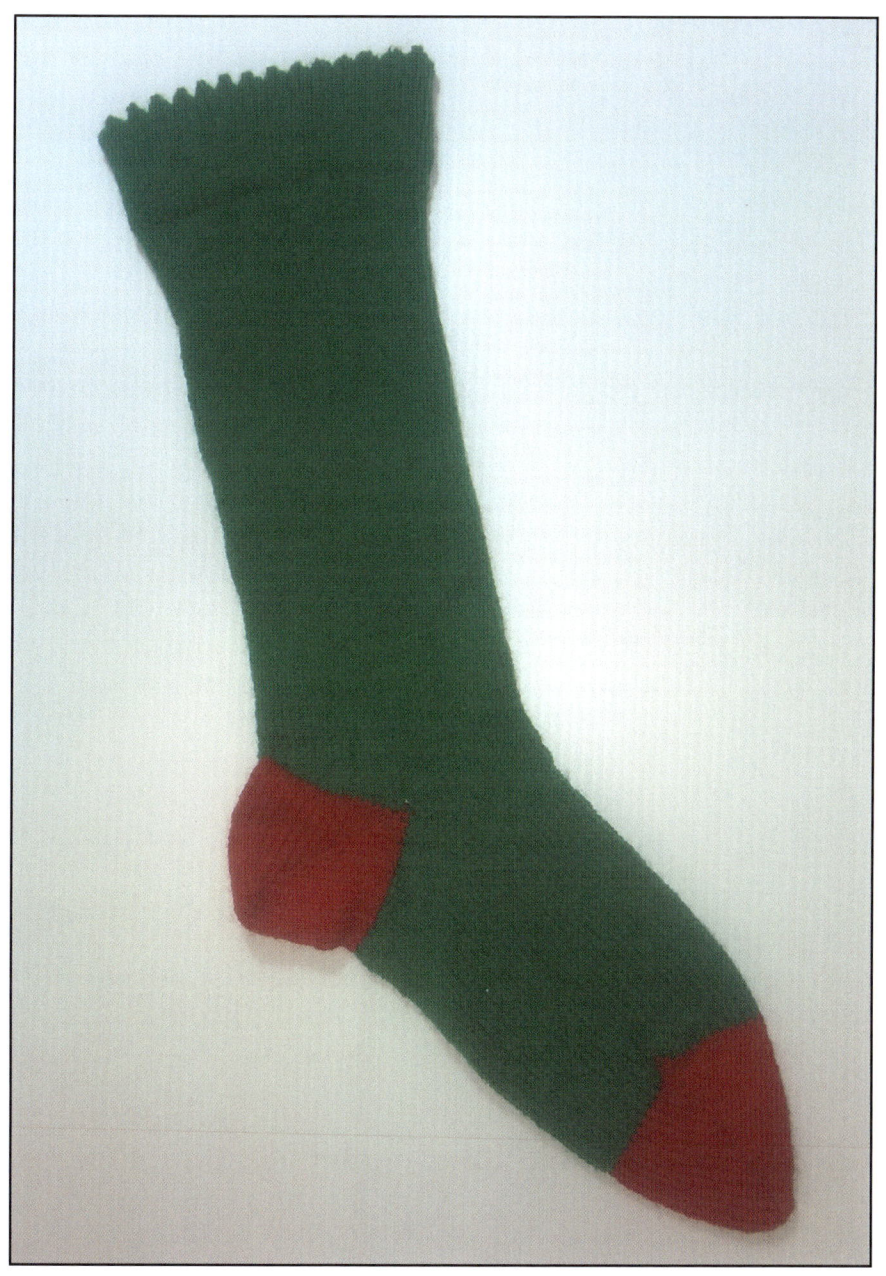

Cast on with waste yarn and knit at least 10 rows (Knit enough rows so that the buckle and weights are in use before beginning the sock.)

Change to sock yarn (right half mark).

Knit 9 rows (count at right half mark).

Knit part of the 10$^{th}$ row, stopping with the yarn carrier in the front of the machine.

Eyelet stitch—transfer the stitch from every other needle to the next needle beginning at the right half mark and moving in the knitting direction. After these stitches have been transferred all the way around the cylinder, knit one round ending at the right half. As with any treatment of an entire row, you will be able to work the transfers most of the way around the cylinder but will reach needles that are not available near the tension cam. Advance the yarn carrier as necessary to complete this eyelet stitch row.

Knit 9 rows (count at right half mark).

Knit part of the 10$^{th}$ row, stopping with the yarn carrier in the front of the machine.

Hang the hem. The first bar after the yarn join goes over the 2$^{nd}$ needle behind (towards the back of the machine) the right half mark. Continue hanging bars, one to a needle, in sequence, in the knitting direction. After all bars have been hung, knit one round ending at the right half mark.

Knit 60 rows. This is the leg from the top of the pre-heel to the welt at the top of the sock. Sock length can be varied according to taste, pattern, and custom measurements. Tension and yarn choices will affect the number of rows required. An approximate length can be determined by measuring the tube inside the sock with the weights removed. The final sock leg will be shorter than the measured web after finishing.

Apply the heel spring and knit 10 rows of pre-heel.

Knit the heel.

Remove the heel spring and knit 40 rows for the body of the sock. Foot length can be varied according to taste, pattern, and custom measurements. Tension and yarn choices will affect the number of rows required. The heel and toe stitches will account for approximately 3 ½ to 4 inches of most finished adult socks.

Knit the toe.

Join waste yarn to the project yarn, leaving at least two feet of project yarn attached for grafting. Pull this tail through to the inside of the tube, and knit waste on all cylinder needles for several rows before beginning the next sock or removing the project from the machine.

Close the toe after removing the sock from the machine.

# 20. HUNG HEM TOP MOCK RIB SOCK

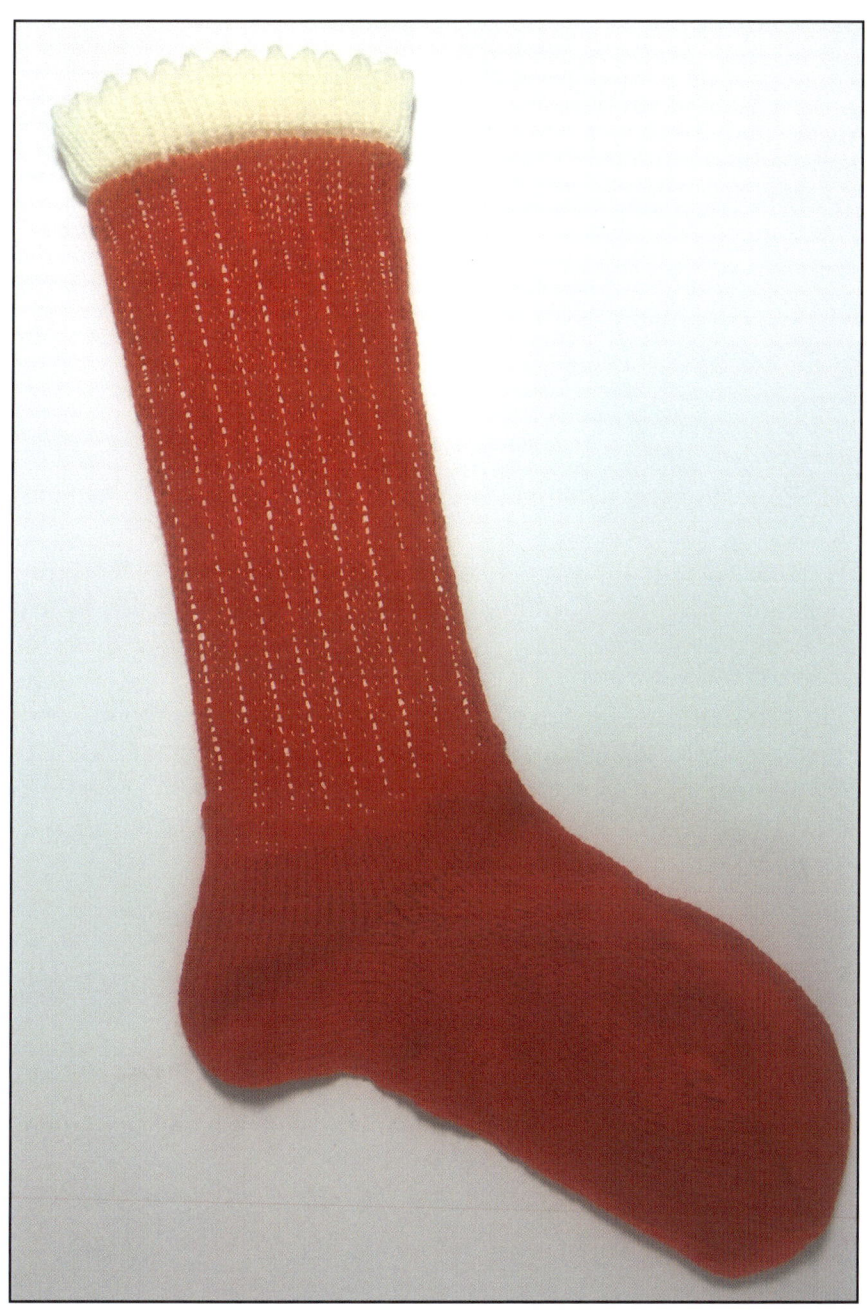

Remove every 4th needle from the machine if the cylinder count can be evenly divided by four (48, 56, 60, 64, 72, 80, 84, 96, 100). Remove every 3rd needle from the machine if the cylinder cannot be evenly divided by four (54).

Cast on with waste yarn and knit at least 10 rows (Knit enough rows so that the buckle and weights are in use before beginning the sock.)

Change to sock yarn (right half mark).

Knit 9 rows (count at right half mark).

Knit part of the 10th row, stopping with the yarn carrier in the front of the machine.

Eyelet stitch—transfer the stitch from every other needle to the next needle beginning at the right half mark and moving in the knitting direction. After these stitches have been transferred all the way around the cylinder, knit one round ending at the right half. As with any treatment of an entire row, you will be able to work the transfers most of the way around the cylinder but will reach needles that are not available near the tension cam. Advance the yarn carrier as necessary to complete this eyelet stitch row.

Knit 9 rows (count at right half mark).

Knit part of the 10th row, stopping with the yarn carrier in the front of the machine.

Hang the hem. The first bar after the yarn join goes over the 2nd needle behind (towards the back of the machine) the right half mark. Continue hanging bars, one to a needle, in sequence, in the knitting direction. After all bars have been hung, knit one round ending at the right half mark.

Knit 60 rows. This is the leg from the top of the pre-heel to the welt at the top of the sock. Sock length can be varied according to taste, pattern, and custom measurements. Tension and yarn choices will affect the number of rows required. An approximate length can be determined by measuring the tube inside the sock with the weights removed. The final sock leg will be shorter than the measured web after finishing.

Replace the needles removed in the first step and put them in the work position. Go as far as you can without moving the yarn carrier and then stop.

Each needle preceding an empty needle has a live stitch hanging and an old stitch below that (the stitch from the previous row). Starting at the right half mark, pick up each old stitch and hang it over each adjacent empty needle, always moving the stitches in the knitting direction.

Move the yarn carrier as necessary to complete this process of adding needles and hanging stitches until all needle slots are filled.

Knit one complete row. Every needle should now be knitting.

Apply the heel spring and knit 10 rows of pre-heel.

Knit the heel.

Remove the heel spring and knit 40 rows for the body of the sock. (Foot length can be varied according to taste or style. Tension and yarn choices will affect the number of rows required. The heel and toe stitches will usually account for approximately 3 ½ to 4 inches.)

Knit the toe.

Join waste yarn to the project yarn, leaving at least two feet of project yarn attached for grafting. Pull this tail through to the inside of the tube, and knit waste on all cylinder needles for several rows before beginning the next sock or removing the project from the machine.

Close the toe after removing the sock from the machine.

The step of hanging stitches from the previous row when needles are added to the machine can be omitted by choice. Needles can be added in sequence and should pick up loops on the first knitting pass, then begin to form true stitches on the second pass. If this option is followed, there will be a slight hole where the knitting begins for each replaced needle. This is not a flaw. It is a design element based on a choice of techniques.

If stitches are hung on the replaced needles, the latches for those needles are most likely to be open, and new stitches should form. If stitches are not hung on these needles, the machine should make a loop around the empty needle on the first pass and begin knitting true stitches on the second. The latch may not be open and should be checked. Some machines are better at forming loops on empty needles than others. If your machine is not consistently forming the loop on the first pass, leave the empty needle raised for one row after it is returned to the machine. Lower the needle before the second row begins. This should establish a loop on the first row and the stitch on the second.

The pre-heel is the ankle area. This process adds the needles before the pre-heel for a solid section of knitting above the heel. An alternative is to add the needles after the pre-heel so that the mock ribs run all the way to the foot. It is unusual to continue mock ribs into the heel, but they may be continued down the length of the top or sides of the foot as desired.

# 21. GENERAL TIPS

Do not reverse the machine unless the yarn carrier is in an area of out of work needles or empty slots.

It is easier to master the knitting process with moderately sized stitches. Extra large and extra small stitches add unnecessary challenges. Practice knitting on the slightly loose side of tension until mastery is achieved, then begin to adjust stitch sizes to suit preferences. *The knitting process itself is a beginner skill. Knitting at tension extremes is an intermediate skill.*

The purposes of the weights are to hold the stitches in the correct place for the needles to create new stitches and to assist the machine to cast off the stitches from the previous row as the new stitches form. You only need enough weight to make this happen. The weights are not intended to elongate or enlarge the stitches. If you are increasing weight to force the machine to knit tight stitches, **STOP!** Adjust your stitch size so that the stitches knit easily. This incorrect method of tensioning with extra weights stresses your machine and may cause many types of failure.

Tension and yarn choices will affect the number of rows required for the various sections of a sock. An approximate length for the finished product can be determined by measuring the tube inside the sock with the weights removed or by calculating the length from a gauge swatch. The final sock will be shorter than the measured web after finishing.

Sampling is necessary to determine the exact numbers of rows required for the chosen cylinder, tension, yarn size, yarn delivery system, and finishing process. *ALL pattern and cylinder charts give approximates. Your results may vary.*

The final sock should be at least ¼ to ½ inches longer than the foot for a good fit. Socks which are snug to the heel and toe will wear out faster than socks that are slightly longer than the foot. The ability to distort the shape of a knit stitch will allow the sock to stretch in one direction with a corresponding decrease in another. While this *is* possible, fitting socks in this manner will cause socks to wear out faster.

The weights distort the shape of the stitches during the knitting process and for varying amounts of time after the project is removed from the machine. The method of finishing will also affect the final product. Do not struggle to knit the project so that it looks like a *finished* sock on the machine.

The amount of humidity in the work area will affect the knitting process and the size of the product. When knitting paired items, attempt to complete them in the same knitting session.

No two machines will work exactly the same way, even if they look identical. This can be very frustrating. Variations in design may require a different approach to settings and techniques. It is helpful to have a manual and/or threading diagram for your specific machine or to work with an individual who is familiar with your model.

There is often more than one method or technique for accomplishing a process. There are many options regarding sock styles and elements. There are many functional machines. You do not have to please anyone else with your choices.

# 22. TERMS AND DEFINITIONS

## MACHINE TERMS

*Back (machine)*: the portion of the machine lying farthest from the knitter when the machine crank is positioned to the knitter's right

*Backward*: reversing direction from that of the most recent knit stitches
  *To knit backwards (stationary cylinder machines)*: advance the yarn carrier clockwise
  *To crank backwards (stationary cylinder machines)*: advance the yarn carrier counter clockwise

*Basic machine*: the portion of the machine required to create knit stitches; the machine without the ribber. Some manufacturers use this term to denote a specific purchase package.

*Crank*: machine part which, when moved, powers the machine
  *To crank*: to make the machine move

*Decrease tension*: to make the stitch larger

*Forward*: continuing to knit in the same direction as the most recent stitches have been knit
  *To knit forwards (stationary cylinder machines)*: advance the yarn carrier counter clockwise
  *To crank forward (stationary cylinder machines)*: to advance the crank handle clockwise

*Front (machine)*: the portion of the machine lying closest to the knitter when the machine crank is positioned to the knitter's right

*Full pitch*: ribber slots aligned with cylinder slots

*Half marks*: cylinder markings that divide the cylinder slots into two equal regions. Usually placed at the sides of the cylinder rather than the front and back. Originals may have been etched or painted.

*Half pitch*: ribber slots offset from cylinder slots

*Hash marks*: cylinder markings—half marks, heel pivot points, and others

*Heel pivots*: cylinder markings identifying the needle which defines the corner between the decrease and increase portions of a short row heel

*In work*: needles which are positioned so that they can make stitches

*Increase tension*: to make the stitch smaller

*Knit*: plain knitting
  *To knit*: to cause the machine to make stitches; may include ribber stitches

*Knob*: rounded top having a threaded shaft; element of the tension adjustment mechanism on the Legare-style machines

*Latch (needle)*: small, movable tongue section of a cylinder or ribber needle
  *Open latch*: a latch or tongue which is positioned so that it does not block the opening of the hook or needle
  *Closed latch*: a latch or tongue which is touching the tip of the hook of the needle and blocking the opening of the hook or needle

*Latch (cam)*: side cam (not commonly used but found in original Gearhart manuals)

*Lower*: return needle to a working position where the needle butt can engage in the relevant cams

*Nut*: threaded collar, possibly incised with numbers; element of the tension adjustment mechanism on the Auto-Knitter/Gearhart/NZAK machines and others

*Out of work*: needles that are positioned so that they will not make stitches. For cylinder needles, out of work needles may be raised so that they are bypassed. For the ribber, a switch may be employed to prevent the needles from moving to collect yarn.

*Pick/hook tool*: hand tool with a fine straight shaft at one end and a crook at the other.

*Raise*: leave cylinder needle in its slot but pull it upward until the needle butt stops against the cylinder spring

*Remove*: take needle out of the machine

*Reverse*: in a broad sense, to make the cam shell revolve clockwise
  *To reverse*: to change the direction of the stitch-making

*Rib*: a vertical course
  *To rib*: to cause the machine to make vertical courses. May be accomplished with an attachment, with a specific sequencing of needles adjacent to empty needle slots, or by direct stitch manipulation

*Slot*: dent or cut designed to hold needle

*Tension*: stitch size or stitch size adjustment
  *To tension*: to change stitch size

*Trick*: dent or cut designed to hold needle

# PRODUCT TERMS

*Cable*: design element in which stitches cross each other to change position within the row

*Course*: stitches lying in successive rows and dependent on each other for structure elements

*Decrease*: to remove a stitch

*Drop*: lose anchor for a stitch, typically the stitch slipping off the needle rather than knitting

*Eyelet stitch*: pattern element created by removing a stitch to an adjacent needle which already contains a stitch, knitting these two together and allowing the empty needle to pick up a loop and continue knitting in later rows. Used for pattern elements and to create a picot edge

*Flat web*: section of knitting which has discrete edges

*Float*: section of yarn joining two stitches

*Increase*: to add a stitch

*Knit*: plain knitting, cylinder stitch
  *To knit*: to cause the machine to make stitches; may include ribber stitches

*Latch*: to create a stitch with a single latch needle powered by hand

*Mock rib*: appearance of vertical courses created by elongating floats. Accomplished by removing needles from the machine and knitting past the empty slots

*Picot*: an edge treatment created by knitting a row of eyelet stitches on every other needle, knitting additional rows, and folding the web at the eyelet to create an edge. Knit together stitches for bumps typical of a picot appearance

*Plain knitting*: also stockinette. Sequential rows of knit stitches with no purl stitches. All stitches present the same face.

*Purl*: stitch in which the loop is drawn backwards through the stitch of the previous row. May be accomplished with an attachment or by direct stitch manipulation
  *To purl*: to create purl stitches. May be accomplished with an attachment or by direct stitch manipulation

*Rib*: a vertical course
　*To rib*: to case the machine to make vertical courses. May be accomplished with an attachment, with specific sequencing of needles adjacent to empty needle slots, or by direct stitch manipulation

*Row*: stitches knit one after another with out reversing or turning or repeating on a previously used needle

*Run*: course of stitches that have unraveled or unknit
　*Run up*: a course of stitches which unravel towards the last knit row
　*Run down*: a course of stitches which unravel towards the earliest knit row

*Selvedge*: treatment or condition which maintains the structural integrity of edge stitches

*Stockinette*: also plain knitting. Sequential rows of knit stitches with no purl stitches. All stitches present the same face

*Tension*: stitch size

*True rib*: vertical courses created by reversed or purl stitches. May be accomplished with an attachment or by direct stitch manipulation

*Tube*: cylindrical section of knitting

*Tuck stitch*: a slipped stitch in one row followed by knitting that same stitch in a successive row. Usually created by raising a needle with a stitch on it out of work, allowing the yarn to knit past it for one or more rows, and then returning the needle to work and allowing it to knit normally

*Web*: the knitting, including purl stitches

*Wrap*: lift yarn and guide it behind one or more needles

# NOTES

# NOTES

# NOTES

Printed in Great Britain
by Amazon